Star Trek

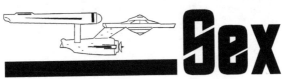

Sex

Star Trek

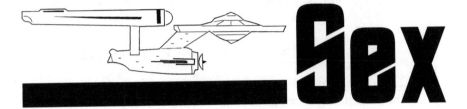

Sex

Analyzing The Most Sexually Charged Episodes of The Original Series

By Will Stape

BearManor Media

2015

Star Trek Sex: Analyzing the Most Sexually Charged
Episodes of the Original Series

© 2015 Will Stape

For information, address:

BearManor Media
P. O. Box 71426
Albany, GA 31708

bearmanormedia.com

Published in the USA by BearManor Media

ISBN—1-59393-862-4
978-1-59393-862-8

For Howard & Robin

America's Sex Life Would Be So Boring Without You

Credit: NBC Television
Copyright: Wikimedia Commons/public domain

"My love has wings, slender feathered things with grace and upswept curve and tapered tip"

– *Nightingale Woman* by
Tarbolde on the Canopus planet

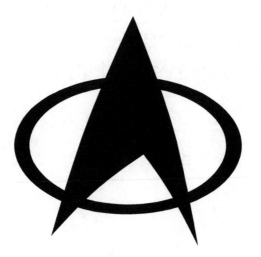

Table of Contents

Foreword

The original *Star Trek* soared high as an entertainment pioneer in many ways. In how it respectfully and seriously treated science, explored important social issues and depicted the inclusion of women and minority groups, and how it proffered the notion of global unification, making it a television and cultural milestone.

Curiously, one important aspect seems to have been mostly overlooked when it comes to examining Gene Roddenberry's *Wagon Train* to the stars—**sex**.

It's true that while the 1960's were exploding with advancements and liberation on all fronts—especially sociological ones - Hollywood and American television still resisted the depiction of graphic physical relations. However, for years, shows like *The Twilight Zone* or *The Outer Limits* could use the vehicle of science fiction to weave a tapestry of entertainment and manage to get more adult themes by the dreaded censors. Writer and producer Gene Roddenberry wanted to do the same with his science fiction program.

So, what is *Star Trek Sex*? This isn't yet another companion, compendium or cross referenced database of planets, props, aliens, trivia or episode synopses. It's not a science manual nor fan fiction romp. It's not a musing on the real science behind the show.

It's all about the sex.

No, it's not a pornographic depiction, nor satire on how love space jockey Captain Kirk handled his many women, or how Spock could maintain multiple boners during his days of heat and lust—the Vulcan Pon Farr.

While going over a large number of original series episodes—thirty seven in all and the feature films, *Star Trek: The Motion Picture* and *Star Trek VI: The Undiscovered Country*—I found that many of the plotlines, character motivations and basic story elements hinged upon or were pre-occupied by sexual expression, lovemaking or good old reliable lust.

Tribbles are such sexually potent and eternally horny creatures they are born pregnant. Orion Slave Girls - those jade skinned beauties—simply reek of dangerous eroticism. Natives from planet Delta IV are so sexually expressive and advanced, they must take an oath of celibacy when dealing with us romance timid humans—since we are so sexually immature compared with those lusty, bald Deltans.

Star Trek may never be confused with the fleshy fantasy of *Barbarella* or pure party atmosphere of *Flash Gordon*, but when it comes to sexuality, it's not just about Captain Kirk's many women. It's about Spock, McCoy, Uhura, Chekov & Scotty loving and losing and others having intense sexual adventures all over the galaxy.

So go and initiate diagnostics, calibrate the dilithium crystal matrix to power up your Kindle, iPad (PADD) or Android tablet or smartphone, and set up in a place with proper mood lighting.

Could Dr. Ruth give sex advice to a lust filled Klingon? Can Dr. Phil help sexually heal a romance rollicking Romulan?

The Human Sexual Adventure Is Just Beginning....

About the Author

Will Stape watched *Star Trek* before he knew the difference between a phaser and a taser. Watching *The Squire of Gothos* (he even remembers the first scene he saw) at around four years of age left such an impression on him that it led him to follow Gene Roddenberry's iconic sci-fi adventure show thereafter.

While attending his first year of college, he became one of a handful of freelance writers to land a script sale to *Star Trek: The Next Generation*. His episode, *Homeward*, guest starring Paul Sorvino (*Goodfellas*), debuted in a prime time slot in the Emmy Award winning TV show's seventh and final season. A year later, he sold another teleplay to *Star Trek: Deep Space Nine*, and saw his script, *Charity*, turned into the Ferengi centric episode, *Prophet Motive*—starring Wallace Shawn (*Princess Bride*).

He's pitched to *Star Trek: Voyager, Deep Space Nine* and met with writer/producer Michael Piller at his production company, Piller Squared, for a pitch meeting for USA Network's hit show, *Stephen King's The Dead Zone*—which Piller had developed and was show runner.

Since then, he's developed docudramas, created TV reality shows and has written extensively for newspapers, magazines, radio and the web for outlets such as: *American Chronicle, Sci-Fi Pulse, Airlock Alpha, McCall's Quilter's Home, Gather, Hudson Reporter, Bayonne Style, Shine, OMG!* and *Yahoo! News & Voices*.

Over the years, he's owned several phasers, but never a taser.

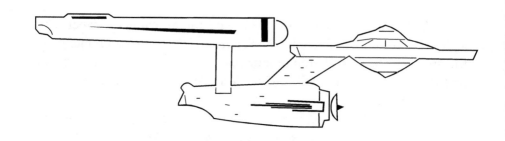

Star Trek Sex

Episodes

The Cage
Situation: Breeding Sex Slaves, Roleplay
Stardate: None Provided

> *Sex: The Feel Good Frontier... These are the sexual positions of the starship Intercourse. Its five year missionary position... to explore strange new sexual adventures... to seek out new hot bodies and new sexuality... to boldly go sexually where no other TV show has gone before...*

Not the *Star Trek* monologue you're used to hearing? Sounds more like a tawdry introduction to one of those home made *Trek* pornos? Yes, it's an easy way to sex up and spoof William Shatner's legendary Captain Kirk monologue. But it's not so jarring nor even gratuitous. When you dig deeper, a frank and adult sexual conversation may not be all that much in conflict with the powerhouse sci-fi franchise.

With *Star Trek: Into Darkness*, from director J.J. Abrams, revising, retelling and reimagining Gene Roddenberry's classic space opera, the sex lives of Zachary Quinto's Spock and his lover Uhura (Zoe Saldana) appear to casual fans as cutting edge or more in line with the more open sexual tone of our times. However, when Starship Enterprise blasted off way back in 1966 on NBC, sexuality was explored often and was much more a part of this TV show than many other television programs from the same era.

The Cage—Too Cerebral or Too Sexually Graphic?
Star Trek's first pilot—the kind of test, proof of concept or premiere episode of a TV series—was called *The Cage*. Starring the first Enterprise

Captain, Jeffrey Hunter (*King of Kings*) as Pike, and produced by Desilu—Lucille Ball's production company—the cosmic outing was rejected by network NBC as being too cerebral (too nerdy?), too slow and too intellectual for them to broadcast. So the network executives did something quite unusual for back then and even today—they ordered another pilot filmed, which would become *Where No Man Has Gone Before*, starring actor Gary Lockwood, most famous for co-starring in director Stanley Kubrick's cinematic masterwork, *2001: A Space Odyssey*.

In the Roddenberry penned story, Pike's Enterprise goes to Talos IV, a planet from where a radio distress call is being transmitted. A group of human survivors are discovered from an exploratory team stranded there for nearly two decades. A young woman named Vina stands out starkly among the small group, since the rest are much older males. Vina is young and incredibly attractive. She exudes a kind of raw sexuality which is impossible for anyone to ignore. Like a mysterious visitor floating in from a libidinous dream state, she fully captures the admiring eyes of Captain Christopher Pike.

When the answer to how a small group of humans without most of the bare necessities could survive years on an alien planet is learned, the sexual tone of the story ramps up to another level. Vastly powerful telepathic aliens, the Talosians, have lured Pike's crew to their planet to enslave the humans and breed them as worker drones or slaves. It's a kind of zoo where the zookeepers encourage and cultivate as much sex as possible, so that their breeding stock will be kept happy and procreate as often as necessary.

Rod Serling's 'The Twilight Zone' Had Susan Oliver First

Back in 1966, the notion of weird aliens—whose make-up made them look more than a little like bare bottoms (real buttheads)—keeping and experimenting with humans as sex slaves appears way too far ahead of its time. Sure, it was the late 60's, and minds and morales were certainly expanding, but for network TV executives, this plotline must have seemed a tad mature. Ironically, several years earlier, Rod Serling's *The Twilight Zone* had an episode in which Roddy McDowall is captured by aliens and put in a zoo. One of the alien zookeepers is none other than Susan Oliver—the actress who played Vina.

The sex escapades of *The Cage* get even more raw and raunchy when the Talosians dial up their telepathic mojo and zap Pike with a near pornographic illusion. They conjure up a den of playful delights where Pike sits at the center of a group of horny men leering and admiring a dancing girl. Vina, slathered from head to toe in jade green skin make-up and dressed in an eye popping, revealing outfit, now whirls around seductively as an Orion slave girl. Her part belly dance, part teasing strip show still smolders as one of the more erotic moments in all of broadcast television. Too cerebral? Too slow? Too intellectual? Really NBC? Or was it all just far too full of sex for your conservative sponsors of 1966?

Human Sexual Mythology

Later, in a more subdued and human themed—albeit stereotypical picaresque—fantasy, Pike finds himself in a pastoral place of great Earth beauty. Vina is now his doting wife or girlfriend, obediently tending to a sumptuous picnic basket, while one of Pike's favorite horses stands nearby. The setting and tone of the Talosian mind trip promotes that of basic human bonding—a happily married couple or young, dynamic dating couple out for fun and frolics in the country for a picnic.

This is entirely convincing simulation on an epic and grandiose scale. It also hearkens to a kind of bizarre alien dating game. Like a speed dating match from hell, the teasing Talosians keep switching up love nests for Captain Pike and Vina.

Another illusion casts Pike as a hero in a kind of sword and sorcery epic, where he must save Vina—now a properly dressed medieval princess—from a rampaging beast. Here again is sexual subtext: Pike's handsome hero, prince or hired sword, saves the fair damsel from the ogre, beast or dragon and takes her off to a wedding night of conquering, celebratory sex. Finally, after Pike keeps resisting the efficacy of the dreamy mind trips to encourage him to have sexual intercourse with Vina, two female Enterprise crew members are captured. One woman the Talosians feel will provide excellent breeding stock for superior intelligence, while the other boasts the physical and biological elements worthy and valuable for the needs of the dastardly aliens.

Right from the first memorable outing, though technically only used later in the two parter *The Menagerie*, *The Cage* charted a mature, near breakthrough course exploring the fascination we all have with human sexuality. While far more tame by today's standards, it impressively sets the stage for one of the most complex and celebrated television explorations of sex. Future spin off shows like *Star Trek: The Next Generation*, *Deep Space Nine*, *Star Trek: Voyager* and *Enterprise* would continue this sociological simulation-like tradition of maturely depicting sexual situations as something more than mere titillation or window dressing. Creator Gene Roddenberry employed the powerful and healthy sexual aspects of ourselves to tell some of the most wondrous stories in the history of television.

Where No Man Has Gone Before
Sexual Situation: Being Frigid, Delusions of Godhood
Stardate: 1312.4

After encountering an old, battered ship's recorder from an Earth space vessel, the SS Valiant, Enterprise approaches and traverses the galactic barrier. The starship is fully enveloped in an immense energy wave, which injures two crewmembers, and also imbues them both with the awe inspiring abilities of a god.

Practice makes perfect. If that's the case, then this 2nd pilot—starring Gary Lockwood and Sally Kellerman (*Back To School*)—is a practiced case of *Star Trek* taking flight and warping straight into entertainment history. NBC accepted the Desilu produced series after this was filmed, and more of the *Star Trek* we came to know and love was evident. Deforest Kelley had not yet assumed the role of Dr. McCoy—here the ship's physician is played by reliable character actor Paul Fix (*The Bad Seed*) and instead of a youthful Russian navigator, Lt Lee Kelso would meet his doom after guiding the starship to planet Delta Vega intent on marooning Mitchell, now transformed into a raging and dangerous godhead.

Mitchell accelerates Dr. Elizabeth Dehner's morph into a superior snob with a nifty bag of parlor tricks to rival Trelane of *Squire of Gothos* or Q from *Encounter At Farpoint*, but he has a motive to his minion mining madness. He wants a partner, a companion—an equal like the Borg Queen would say—to sit next to him on a self made, royal throne presiding over a lonely, desolate world. He wants a mate.

In the first act, Gary Mitchell tosses off a crack which not only sets the tone for the rest of the rollicking tale, but infuses the story with a sense of focused gender competition. After Dr. Dehner rebuffs Mitchell's advances, he bitterly quips, "Walking freezer unit that one."

Frigid. It's one of those unflattering, politically incorrect terms that we all cringe at today, but its social acceptance or casual, colloquial usage isn't as important as the look it gives into Gary Mitchell's male dominated sense of self. Later, when Kirk is talking to what's left of his friend—in terms of his base humanity now lost—they reminisce about their wild exploits on Deneb IV. Mitchell mentions a romantic one, commenting, "Yeah, she was nova that one." *A walking freezer unit. A nova (hot) one.* Apparently, Mitchell likes temperature extremes when considering the potential romantic assessment of his women.

After piercing the galactic barrier, Dr. Dehner becomes fascinated with Mitchell because of his abilities and high ESP rating. Dehner starts to succumb to Mitchell's intense romantic flirtations—but is it because he's suddenly become her type, or because of the mind blowing metaphysical condition they both now share? Sexual or psychic lure?

Credit: NBC Television
Copyright: Wikimedia Commons/public domain

While being examined in sickbay, Mitchell boasts he's read the entirety of the Enterprise's knowledge tapes. Dehner quizzes him and he reads back to her a passionate love poem, "My love has wings, slender, feathered things with grace in upswept curve and tapered tip." He points out to her that the passage she had him remember was regarded as one of the most passionate love sonnets of the last few centuries.

In the episode's final act, Mitchell and Dehner are now standing together almost as one—equal in power—their humanity nearly vanished, replaced by eerie glowing eyes and an awesome ability to conjure up virtually any wish at will. Even here, when anything is at his command or desire, Mitchell acts more like a lovesick school boy with a massive crush—or even creepier, and by today's criminal standards—he's a kind of uber powerful stalker with supreme omnipotence as his allure.

One thing is clear to us at the close of this tragic tale: If Gary Mitchell hadn't been tempted by his very human sexuality, he'd never have brought Dehner over to join him in his self aggrandized rank and irresistible godly power. It is she who ultimately tips the balance of power in Kirk's favor. So, at the final and most important moment, his volcanic sexual proclivities have laid him bare and vulnerable; he's completely helpless to resist her, and he ends up being oh so very human and weak—while reveling in our lowly human wants and ungodly physical appetites.

The Man Trap
Sexual Situation: Trans-species Sex, Rekindled Romance—Denial
Stardate: 1513.1

> *When Enterprise travels to planet M-113, Dr. McCoy gives medical exams to a married couple—one a respected archaeologist, Dr. Robert Crater, and his wife, Nancy. She's a woman Bones has carried a torch for, and he hasn't laid eyes on her in many years. After Starfleet officers start dying off at the hands of a brutal killer, it's theorized that Nancy isn't at all who she appears to be—but is in reality a vampire-like shape shifting creature who feeds off the salt found in humans.*

What if you were reunited with your long lost love and she or he hadn't aged a day since your break-up? Even more surprising—and certainly more than titillating—what if she or he could assume the physical appearance of anyone? They could be a different lover to you each and every night. You could experience a never ending range of partners with differing physical gifts and never be stung by the debilitating guilt of cheating on them with another. Dr. McCoy faces this prospect when he's forced to re-examine his feelings for a woman he cared for and hasn't seen in a decade.

The Salt Creature or Salt Vampire remains one of *Star Trek's* most fascinating and recognizable creatures. Despite the old school FX achieved through a suit and make-up—or perhaps because of it—the hairy, leech-like beast strikes a chord like few other alien beasts from Roddenberry's creature galaxy. With a mouth reminiscent of a suckerfish or catfish, and spindly fingers complete with octopus like suction cups, the predatory thing shocks us as weird, cool and scary. Like so many other incredible visuals, it was created by the great artist Wah Chang (*The Outer Limits*)—who also created the communicator, modified the iconic phaser and crafted the nifty tricorder props.

The creature's shape shifting element—to be seen again in Garth of Izar in *For Whom Gods Destroy*, all the way up to Iman's shifting traitor from the Klingon prison in *Star Trek VI: The Undiscovered Country*, plays well in a story about lost or unrequited love. After all, no matter how much time passes, don't we all see ourselves and our loved ones almost exactly as we both co-existed with one another in our loving and comforting prime? In our minds and most of all in our protecting hearts, age takes no toll and has no place to reside.

When it's revealed that Dr. Crater's real wife—and McCoy's one time flirtation—was killed off by the creature years ago, who now assumes her form to please him, the revelation that the archaeologist tolerates and even relishes this creepy charade is both bewildering and skin crawling. It sounds like the kinky scholar participates in a physical or even sexual masquerade with the alien salt feeder. Does Crater trade salt for affection, companionship or even interspecies sex? It's never said aloud nor confirmed by him, but what else could the two be doing there alone on the planet for all those many years? Indeed, it gives new meaning to the concept of an interracial romantic pairing—this one is an *interspecies* love affair.

For McCoy's part, he too feels torn up internally. His human mind isn't so nimble nor capable of accepting the fact that his beloved Nancy is truly dead and this salt sucker has replaced her like a body snatcher. Like some of the dead eyed humans who see their loved ones become zombies on AMC's *The Walking Dead*, it's easy for one to deny the truth when it's so damn unreal.

This sodium chloride addicted changeling can so thoroughly deceive a lovesick man like Leonard McCoy, that not even Spock double fisting punching her in the face—*one of the episode's coolest, most memorable scenes*—can sway him quickly enough to act in defense of his superior officer, Captain Kirk. Nancy brings down Kirk as if he were a weak boy, and then easily disables the Vulcan Spock, who's desperately trying to save his Captain and convince Bones of the reality of the dire situation. Finally, McCoy acts and kills the salty creature with a phaser.

Leonard McCoy is a man who found his love again, only to lose her to his own hand. He was forced to kill something that had so fully captured a woman from his past, that he nearly let his Captain and friend be killed in front of him. How could Dr. McCoy be that deceived or slow in acting—to wake up to the truth? Maybe, in the end, in that moment of reckoning, in that split second decision making moment, he didn't want to face up to the truth. Was he like Data in *Star Trek: First Contact*—telling Picard that he hesitated, albeit so briefly, when considering the Borg Queen's offer to make him into a human being?

The salt creature didn't merely copy a woman, nor bring McCoy back to the Nancy he knew and loved, it did something much more powerful and enticing. It plucked the best, the most vibrant and the most romantic image and beloved memory from his brain to create a woman who could never be equaled in flesh and blood reality. It exploited that weakness we all have when it comes to the ones we love—especially those we love romantically. The most tender, most passionate and most stimulating moments we share with our lovers mix deep feelings and tumultuous emotions like no other. The salt vampire exploited this and thereby bought itself years of life with Dr. Crater, and nearly escaped extermination and almost escaped death again because of Dr. McCoy's human hesitation and his physical, sexual weakness and biological fallibility.

Charlie X
Sexual Situation: Puberty
Stardate: 1533.6

> *When the Enterprise crew is entrusted with the safekeeping and priority transport of a young human male, little do they realize he's been given awesome powers of matter replication, manipulation and teleportation, enabling him to will nearly anything he*

desires into existence, or remove things (including people) from our dimension and spirit them away. To utterly confound and compound things: this near god is basically still just a boy.

Charlie Evans always wants his own way, and he seems to always get it. He's a spoiled, bratty teen fresh from adolescence emergence, and he expects everything to be given to him now—the curse of instant gratification inherent in the impatience of youth. But he's never met someone like the commander of the Starship Enterprise. He's now met his match in the uber-like symbol of 23rd century masculinity – Captain James T. Kirk.

Charles Evans is a young man without much of a plan. The only thing he has going for him—and it's certainly a big thing—is the ability to do almost anything by just thinking about it. So, what's exactly the matter with Mr. Evans? If you can do anything, why aren't things going swimmingly for the teenager?

One word: *Puberty.*

Remember your first kiss? Or how about, the more accurate experience for many of us, your first *attempt* at a kiss. How about recalling the first time you went out on a real date—without friends or anybody else hanging around or watching your attempt to *score*. Remember all these things, and also recall how awkward, hyperactive and all thumbs you were because you were still going through puberty—the tumultuous change from childhood to semi-adulthood. This is the reason Mr. Evans is so at odds with the world around him—but most of all, he's in conflict with himself.

Like Gary Mitchell before him, Charles—or Charlie as the crew call him—will stop at nothing to see his desires carried out in the extreme. Most of all, his desire is a romantic one for an Enterprise crewmember. He goes from displaying a boyish, endearing flirtation to a near insatiable lust for Yeoman Janice Rand, played by Grace Lee Whitney.

One of the most enjoyable plot points, and one that rings most true, is Charlie's need to have Kirk mentor him. It starts out innocently and naturally. As the starship's leader, Captain Kirk is the appropriate man to look to as a role model. But as the tale progresses, even though Charlie still wants his own way and is ruthless about how to achieve his goals, he clearly yearns for an older brother or parental symbol of Kirk to shepherd him through this chaotic time of change.

Perhaps, in a dark and subconscious place he doesn't dare to reveal, he even wants Kirk to somehow cure him of this curse—to yank out the alien gifts which enable him to be godlike, so that he may revert to just being a teenage boy reunited with humans and pining away helplessly for Yeoman Rand. Spock talks about Charlie's need to be led or even disciplined by the Captain, but there's a notion of wanting to also simply be a human being again—not a sideshow mutant freak.

Much like Gary Mitchell, Charlie's unrestrained hunger—his sexual appetite—is the thing which seems to do him in at the end. When the aliens come back to reclaim their adopted son, they're dismayed and disappointed at Charlie's misdeeds. Charlie has so abused the great powers they bestowed on him by trivializing his abilities and abusing the Enterprise crew. Above all the slights he faces, Janice Rand rejects Charlie and this causes him to wish her away, and to then ramp up his steely resolve to take over the Enterprise and drive it to wherever he wishes—he's a super powered teen jockeying out on the most ultimate of cosmic joyrides.

It's a heart rending moment when Charlie is taken back by the alien race which made him into this Frankenstein-like magic monster. It's a palpable experience as he wails mournfully and explains to the human crew—these beings can't be held or can't or will not *love*. They simply don't have the loving emotional underpinnings of the human race. So because of Charlie's rush to be a man—to overcome his fears, his hesitations and to satisfy the raging libido which all teenagers have, he's doomed to live out his life in a limbo-like dimension in the company of soulless beings who cannot return the love he so desperately craves and needs.

The Naked Time
Sexual Situation: Hedonism, Romantic Love Confessionals
Stardate: 1704.2

> *After discovering a group of deceased research scientists on a remote planet in its death throes, the Enterprise crew picks up a kind of inebriation inducing water molecule bug. As it's passed from person to person, its debilitating side effect is much like being completely smashed drunk. What follows are comedic, dramatic and dangerous situations with a crew gone completely out of rational control.*

Ever go out on a wild bender with friends and find yourself in places and with people you would never have interacted with while sober? Think of the kooky craziness of *The Hangover* meeting *Star Trek*, and it's a sense of the crazy ride the crew of Enterprise NCC-1701 take while essentially falling over themselves smashed drunk on a buggy water molecule. The clever plot device gives the *Star Trek* actors a chance to fully spread their thespian wings and show off just how emotionally versatile and broadly they can project with their characters.

Highlights include: Sulu prancing around with his sword like Bruce Lee meets The Three Musketeers D'artagnan, Lt. Kevin Riley showing off his sad lack of singing talent by butchering the classic Irish folk song, "I'll Take You Home Again, Kathleen", while others jump around and laugh constantly or cry incessantly. Remind you of the many dive bars and pubs you've frequented? Sure, we all can relate, either in our reckless youth, or perhaps in a more embarrassing reliving of hard party days. *The Hangover* vibe is what makes this one so much fun. The human power of sexuality, and in this case the Half Vulcan libido, also comes strongly into play.

Majel Barrett—Gene Roddenberry's later wife in real life—portrayed Nurse Chapel, Dr. McCoy's reliable nurse. As a medical professional, Chapel was a competent medical crackerjack, but did she succeed in hiding her passion for a certain alien hybrid member of the crew? Not so much. Her confession comes courtesy of the alcohol-like water molecule, so some could say it's suspect, even influenced by the virus-like booze bug, but Chapel's pining for the half Human, half Vulcan would become an arc throughout the TV series.

During the poignant confessional, Chapel transmits the boozy liquor-like chemical to Spock, whose Vulcan/Human constitution soaks it up and it acts upon his magnificent computer-like mega brain. In short order, he's reduced to a flow of tears which builds to a raging river.

He becomes a sobbing wreck of a man—blubbering about how he was so closed off emotionally he could never tell his human mother that he loved her. When Kirk tries to get his officer off his whining butt and back to his Starfleet duty, the Captain is promptly infected and he goes off like a rocket man of emotions, questioning his leadership abilities as a Starship commander and displaying a slight persecution complex.

The title suggests a baring of one's soul completely, and despite the more comic bits like Riley auditioning like one of Simon Cowell's mocked rejects on *American Idol* or *X-Factor*, the revelations about Nurse Christine Chapel's romantic desires for Spock set the stage for a lovely dramatic dance the characters would engage in over the years—and into the motion pictures. In *Star Trek: The Next Generation*, a sequel—at least in tone—episode called *The Naked Now* plays with revealing Captain Picard's crew's vulnerable character moments. It includes one of the most sexually frank expressions one character has for another, when Tasha Yar recruits the android Data as her own personal sex toy.

Sexually programmable in multiple techniques indeed!

The Enemy Within

Sexual Situation: Psychosexual, Hedonism, Sexual Predator & Pathological Behavior
Stardate: 1672.1

> *While exploring planet Alpha 177, a transporter accident splits Captain Kirk into two distinct men. One remains still civilized and uses his higher reasoning to continue to function as Enterprise Commander, the other shocks as a primitive minded, raging and living example of Freud's concept of the Id. Time is running out—both for the away team marooned on a frozen planet, and the divided Captains, who are now devolving into more extreme versions of their base selves.*

Dr. Jekyll and Mr. Hyde. Larry Talbot and Wolfman. The Hulk and Bruce Banner.

The complex duality of the average human personality may not be as pronounced as these literary, Hollywood and comic book anti-heroes, but we all struggle with a sense of a divided self—at least at some point in our lives. Sprouting a dense forest of body hair and a nightmare overbite, bursting out of your clothes in a jade green roid rage, or downing a beaker of a potion and morphing into a hedonistic ogre is fun stage and screen sci-fi drama. *Hulk Smash!*

James T. Kirk is not unlike any other hyper motivated, physically attractive, statistic shattering and brilliant Starship Captain. In fact, considering others made from the same mold like Captains Picard, Pike, Sisko and Janeway, it takes one highly disciplined individual—constantly in control of one's emotions and impulses—to save planetary civilizations, negotiate with vastly more intelligent entities, and romance so many dynamic people. Despite that tightly maintained exterior, it doesn't mean there isn't a chaotic, even self serving man or woman floating right below the surface just waiting to pop out. Apparently, the trick to exploiting such a Type A personality for forging a successful career is to exert a tremendous force of balance over one's baser instincts.

Ambitious explorers blessed with wanderlust must possess no small amount of hunger for life—a hearty appetite to fuel their burning curiosity and spur them on to great, even historic discoveries. Take Paul Walker, the Hollywood actor from *The Fast And Furious* movies. Walker loved speed, he loved moving fast—it wasn't just a fictional character expression for him. His pursuit of high speed vehicles on and off the silver screen contributed to his fame and fortune, and sadly, it appears to have led to his untimely death in a tragic car accident.

When Kirk is divided by the transporter—that fun, though wildly unpredictable plot convenient tech gadget—the 'good' Kirk seems to be able to get along without having access to the 'bad' Kirk. As the tale wears on, we find that the good, good Captain Kirk can't really balance out his complex life as the leader of Starfleet's flagship, and arguably its most important vessel. He needs the rough edge of his personality—the man's man that tempers the softer side of his persona. In today's parlance, he needs to access his *bitch* within.

So, now that we've properly renamed the episode in observance of today's tone and cadence, *The Bitch Within* marks not only an engaging adventure for Kirk and his fans—albeit more of a mental one bubbling up within himself—but it also is one of the more honest character explorations *Star Trek* offers. We may not like our own *bitch* within—we may knock it unconscious temporarily, bury it for awhile and even wholly deny its existence, but we know we all possess that primal, raging bitch that allows us to conquer our quieter selves and to even survive life's more trying moments.

Sexual domination and submission—the duality of the multi-faceted human libido—celebrates the dominant kind of man the 'bad' Kirk shows himself to be. When he breaks into Yeoman Rand's quarters and struggles with her, he's clearly attempting to satisfy his most violent sexual urges. This raw moment frightens us as a possible rape of the beautiful Rand, and when she savagely scratches him and sends him off running, we know that if she hadn't acted so quickly and defensively, things may have turned out quite differently.

In the end, the Yin Yang of Kirk's personality is fully restored and the Enterprise has her Captain back. Of all the crewmen who had to deal with the 'bad' Kirk, we know undoubtedly Yeoman Janice Rand can never forget the sexual predator who nearly violated her. Like many sad and frightening cases of date rape or sexual violation committed by a friend or family member on a victim, it's something which will probably always linger in the back of Rand's mind.

When you closely examine this heady trip into the dark corners of one man's mind, you realize the upgrade of the title by renaming it *The Bitch Within* is not only easy fun, it's really quite appropriate. For while the 'bad' Kirk may have been naughty, he was no enemy—as we see, Kirk needs him at the end. He was merely operating under the complex personality umbrella of the bitch mode, which we all will have experienced.

Mudd's Women
Sexual Situation: Fantasy Escort Service, Prostitution, Pimping
Stardate: 1329.8

Meet the irrepressible Harry Mudd. He's an entrepreneur who deals in the most profitable of all exploitative trades—the human sexual appetite. When the Enterprise rescues the scheming Mudd and his alluring female passengers from their doomed cargo ship, Captain Kirk and crew must deal with a trio of young women who are irresistibly sexually attractive to all males who encounter them.

Escort services—basically fancier, high priced prostitution—deal in the convenient and discreet companionship for well heeled customers. The working girls—or guys—can effectively court clients with high minded, low brow, or plain weird fantasy in mind. Like some modern, western version of an exotic Geisha from Japan, the escort, call girl, gigolo or prostitute enables a wealthy client to feel a bond that's not really there. Certainly, the physical aspects of skilled sexuality is something most anyone can practice and eventually become adept at, but the more intangible—that indefinable extra—which the truly superstar sex worker deals in isn't common nor easy to achieve or maintain. Some would say a skilled prostitute is more Oscar worthy than some of the Hollywood A-List thespians who win the golden guy.

Harcourt Fenton Mudd—to his beloved wife, Stella, Harry to his friends and those he does business (or bilks) with—fancies himself as a one man escort service. Today, he'd just be known simply as a pimp. Since he's a man who doesn't like to leave much to chance, he won't simply rely on the natural charms of his bevy of beauties. So, to satisfy the sci-fi angle of Roddenberry's Wagon Train To The Stars, Mudd was a pimp and also a drug pusher. Instead of making his girls shoot up heroin, snort cocaine or take meth, he gives them the Venus Drug—a kind of powerful, narcotic love potion.

Not only does the Venus Drug imbue a sexual quality about Mudd's women, it apparently creates the illusion of the taker being more youthful and more sexually desirable. The Venus Drug may not be *Love Potion Number 9*; evidently it's better, but becomes mentally if not physically addictive.

At the tale's finale, Kirk gives Eva a fake Venus Drug fix—to see if it can fool both her body and mind. This encourages a placebo effect in the dejected Eva and frees her self confidence. She's now able to attract those around her more for the way she carries herself and, for lack of a better term, her *inner beauty*. The ugly duckling has sworn off her pusher's fix and instead of scoring narcotics in the future, she'll simply project a Dr. Phil or Tony Robbins level of self confidence and awareness to get through life.

It's a bit storybook, or even pollyanna to those of us who well know that life usually treats the most physically attractive of us better than those with wanting looks. Study after study finds that something as basic and important as a job interview can rest heavily on how physically attractive one is. We may not have to be supermodels or dashing actors to land that job, but it sure helps things.

Still, the lesson is a good one—be yourself—don't rely on the external or the artificiality to get through life. Wouldn't it be nice and certainly refreshing to see the actors and actresses of today's Hollywood take that advice and practice it. They'd all shun the artificial facelifts, surgery, botox and collagen injections and be themselves. The Venus Drug may have been an invention of *Star Trek*, but its surgical analog appears to be real—alive and well in scores of our silver screen stars.

What Are Little Girls Made Of?
Sexual Situation: Rekindle romance, artificial human sexuality
Stardate: 2712.4

When Nurse Chapel is reunited with her old love, Dr. Roger Corby, the Doctor's demeanor appears as cold, even frigid, as the frozen planet his remote lab is located on. It's soon revealed Corby—with the assistance of advanced and ancient alien technology—wants to start replacing people with androids so lifelike, most anyone would be fooled by them. His first test of the alien tech? Captain Kirk.

Google is making waves by ramping up the technology they offer to the masses—or at least invest in and experiment with to advance what will be commercially available to consumers in the future. From their cool to look at—though clunky to display while wearing—Google Glass, the **Google Goggles** as it were, to absorbing robotics companies into their Borg-like collective, the motto 'Don't be evil' could be changed to 'The Robots Are Coming'. We hope they aren't evil. For now, the robots they've helped create aren't exactly like the Brent Spiner portrayed Lt. Cmdr. Data in *TNG*, nor the Haley Joel Osment's portrayal of a little boy android in the Kubrick and Spielberg collaboration, *A.I.*, but what happens when they manage to get close to that or even go beyond? Will we welcome androids or reject them?

It's a safe bet, considering the robots and artificial constructs which already populate our society, the universal acceptance of ubiquitous and servile, and more humanoid-like machines will be somewhere in the middle. I'd like to think it will be reminiscent of how George Lucas painted his culture of droids in *Star Wars*. These machines—including types like C3PO and R2D2—are tolerated, even valued, but they're not truly loved nor reviled. They simply exist to serve humans. They're tools—like a buzz saw, skateboard or laser scalpel—bought, sold and traded as would be a used car or a lawn mower.

One area explored in the Spielberg directed *A.I.* was the frank portrayal of physical pleasure in the form of sex androids. These synthetic sex workers—dramatized and portrayed as one by British actor Jude Law—handled the more modern sexual appetites of human culture. In *What Are Little Girls Made Of*, the beautiful Andrea seems to come close to cybernetic prostitution or could act in such a capacity. Ruk, the towering Ted Cassidy from *Addams Family* fame, appears to be the bouncer, security or bodyguard model. Since he was created directly by the 'old ones', his powers and abilities are undoubtedly far more flexible in all respects.

The Achilles heel of Corby—or of someone seeking to intentionally make a machine more human-like, say as Dr. Soong did with Data and Lore—is how human his man to machine transfer is when it does its cyber voodoo. It infuses his memories and even feelings, after a fashion, to his android form, yet the color and texture isn't always replicated in full. It certainly can't be heralded as a complete, convincing replica of a human being. There seems to be something—that indefinable—missing from the human equation.

"We human beings are full of unpredictable emotions, which logic cannot solve." When Kirk says this to Ruk, we know despite the most advanced computer technology—even in that fantastic, futuristic time—Kirk is right about the variable randomness of our human emotional condition. But it is the beautiful android Andrea who fully embraces humanity's illogical sexuality, setting the stage for Corby's downfall.

When Andrea—urged on by the real Kirk—tries to get the android Kirk to engage in a kiss, his rejection doesn't sit well with her. She wastes little time in firing a phaser to destroy the clever Corby construct. Finally, when all is revealed—when Corby is found out to be an android himself, the synthetic doctor explains he had his mind carried over into the sturdy artificial body. Chapel can't deal with such high tech chicanery. She completely rejects such an inhuman solution to death, and that's when Andrea pounces. Her android personality can indeed love, but when Andrea admits her passion for him, Corby—still despairing over Chapel's rejection of him no doubt—destroys himself and Andrea with a phaser. Andrea's too human need for a passionate physical, sexual response doomed the Corby android.

Miri

Sexual Situation: Puberty Triggers Genetic Disorder Causing Insanity & Death
StarDate: 2713.5

> *Enterprise's finest must deal with precocious kids and teenagers on an alien world, who are infected with a genetic disorder causing death in adults and targeting youth during the onset of puberty. While an infected away team, including Captain Kirk, Spock and McCoy, race to find a cure, a girl named Miri balances her schoolgirl-like crush for Kirk with her allegiance to a ragtag band of kids who are slowly growing up and becoming infected themselves.*

Puberty is awkward. It can be clumsy. It can hurt. It's funny to almost all but the poor guy or gal going through it. Here, on this strange new world, puberty can literally be deadly. It's a literal depiction of the many difficult maturation stages a girl or boy goes through to become an adult. Nobody ever said growing up would be easy or fair.

No matter how advanced our present age is with medical assistance, we can all remember just how hard it was to grow up. The gangly physical changes we suffered, the bizarre vocal adjustments—not to mention the huge influx of hormones and the powerful crushes which turned into raging passionate affairs—at least in our erotically charged minds or confided in with our BFFs. Would there really be a tomorrow? Would we live to see adulthood—out there in the distance, beckoning us on to assume maturity?

For the seemingly innocent girl Miri and the others of her doomed race, puberty doesn't simply mean social and personal struggle—it means death. Long ago, her people experimented with genetic technology and managed to prolong her race's life by centuries —but the trade-off was creating and contracting a debilitating, deadly disease once the infected victim moved from puberty into adulthood. Raging insanity and eventual death awaited them.

Now, her and about a dozen 'kids' scrounge around a western style ghost town, playing childish games and talking about how bad the 'grups' are—a contraction of grown-ups. The sheer creepiness of the whole scene is that Miri and her fellow kids aren't kids at all—at least chronologically. In reality, they're hundreds of years older—their age slowed drastically by the dreaded disorder which will eventually kill them once puberty passes and the maturity of adulthood takes hold of them.

The stakes get higher with the arrival of the Enterprise crew. An away team beams down and is soon attacked by what appears to be a mutated creature. It's violent in its savage attack, but when physically restrained becomes pitiful to Kirk, Spock and McCoy as it whines and cries about its broken bicycle as would a child. The creature appears more to be a mentally challenged minor, bereft of the social skills or mental acuity to communicate effectively with strangers. After it thrashes about and dies violently, the Starfleet officers know something is amiss.

When Miri appears on the scene, and starts to flirt with Kirk, the Captain realizes he must tread lightly around so vulnerable a young woman. Even an adult with a solid background, emotional experience and constitution to weather as stressful a situation as what Miri and her peers are facing, would be tasked and challenged to keep it all together and remain sane. That she is essentially a 300 year old teenager, without the mental tools to deal with the consequences of a crush which could really hurt her, makes gentleness necessary.

The complex themes of *Miri* illustrate a subtext which tells us puberty is highly stressful, completely transformative and could even be dangerous. It may not be literally deadly, in the most common experiences of the average person, but the things it brings with it—dating, committed romantic relationships and the risks inherent with such adult behavior—can indeed bring injury upon one, or even worse.

The Return of the Archons
Sexual Situations: Hedonism, Orgies
StarDate: 3156.2

> *After a mentally disturbed Sulu beams up from planet Beta III, Captain Kirk and an away team retrace his steps to investigate what happened to him. A century earlier, the Starship USS Archon was lost after visiting the same planet. Now, Enterprise must deal with a zombie-like populace under the tyrant-like influence of a mysterious being called Landru, who allows his usually law abiding citizens to become hedonistic hellions doing anything they please during a frightening period of time called Festival.*

Summer of 2013 saw the release of an intriguing sci-fi horror movie called *The Purge*. Starring Ethan Hawke (*Gattaca*), and helmed by director James DeMonaco, the low budget movie—made for around $3 million dollars—hit the box office hard and generated almost $90 million in profit. The movie posited the extreme notion of implementing a social program in a future USA, where the government sets aside one day out of the year to allow its populace to commit most any crime without punishment. In theory, it keeps crime way down, since everyone would be 'saving up' time, energy and weaponry for their big crime come the merry Purge day. I suppose the logic behind it is like the celebrating of Christmas Day or Halloween—you wouldn't hang your stockings in February, dress up as Dracula or Iron Man just any day of the week, nor go trick or treating in May. It's a one day party.

Similarly, during the time of Festival, the Beta III citizens run around like sugar high hyperactives, or drunk or wasted *Beliebers* at a Justin Beiber concert. Well, kinda sorta like that, they certainly run around and scream like Beiber buddy babies. They smash and break windows with big rocks or their shoes or whatever. They go around and punch people randomly, and they engage in wanton and spontaneous sexual activity. Most disturbingly of all, perhaps, they seem to also engage in brutal rape and even murder.

In the 1967 episode, owing to the more conservative time and broadcast nature, we never see actual footage of graphic sexuality, but there are plenty of suggestions—and even quick cuts of men grabbing a hold of women and firmly planting kisses on them. We don't see what happens after that, but it's probably safe to assume that they aren't simply going to go for a long walk to discuss what a cool and neat leader Landru is to them.

That Landru is ultimately discovered to be no more than a convincing hologram, floating about with his deep bass voice bugging people, and generated by a long forgotten supercomputer, caps a nifty tale with the kind of Big Brother social system *Star Trek* is well known for exploring. Here, the Landru which rules the planet is a mere shadow and tech reflection of either a long dead ruler, scientist or philosopher. His personality persists in digital form—to ensure his people have a social venting for their more primal proclivities.

Ultimately, the plot plays out like a cautionary tale against a nation or world suppressing the vice-like appetites of its populace. Beta III people operate in a quasi limbo where no manner of fun or pleasure is accepted or encouraged. Their wardrobe is also a clue to the tone of the social intricacies surrounding them. They waltz around in 19th century, Victorian or Amish inspired garb, making them even more the poster people for a time linked to the suppression or full burying of one's physical and sexual desires.

Imagine a time or place in our own reality where sexual freedoms were all but taken away from us as Americans, or in any free minded country. One only has to go back a few decades to recall that many things we take for granted now concerning a healthy and open nature of human sexuality were nowhere to be found. Before Dr. Ruth, before Dr. Drew's love lines, before Dr. Phil—even before Dr. Joyce Brothers—human sexuality was looked upon as private parts—a secret taboo to be rarely discussed. In Landru's world, we can see just how far we've come as a sexually healthy society, where the expression of romantic love isn't cloaked in those old puritanical robes.

Space Seed
Sexual Situation: Submission & Domination
StarDate: 3141.9

After Enterprise encounters the Earth sleeper ship Botany Bay, long slumbering and genetically enhanced humans are released from suspended animation hibernation chambers. When it's learned the leader of the group is the infamous Khan Noonien Singh, an Earth despot responsible for the murder and torture of scores of people, Kirk must engage in battle a man who is his equal or better, for the very command of his Starship.

Summer 2013 blockbuster *Star Trek: Into Darkness* gave the sci-fi cinema world Khan back. Well, in essence anyway, because the Khan we ultimately got wasn't portrayed by a Latin actor, unlike in *Space Seed* and the iconic feature film *Star Trek II: The Wrath of Khan*, in which Ricardo Montalban (*Fantasy Island*) handled the role. Benedict Cumberbatch, best known for playing Sherlock Holmes in the UK, is an English actor. Not only was Khan changed around in terms of look—and obvious ethnic heritage—but he was, for lack of a better word, made wimpy.

Oh, Cumberbatch's Khan efficiently, even theatrically, roars grandiose threats at Kirk and others and sputters off loads of not so memorable lines. He always does this loudly with a great bass voice. Cumberbatch is known for his practiced and powerful voice, as he provides the thunderous vocal magic for Smaug in *The Hobbit* films. He also does his best to viciously beat up the adrenalin pumped, Vulcan strong Spock played by Zach Quinto (*Heroes*), as though the two were dual auditioning for membership in the Avengers, X-Men or Brotherhood of Evil Mutants. Khan scoring in the fiery romance department? Not so much. There's nothing romantic nor of magnetic romance about the newly imagined Khan, but that's not how it was with the original. Montalban's Khan was charismatic with everyone who met him, but he was especially influential over the ladies—one in particular.

Lt. Marla McGivers (Madlyn Rhue) is a woman who's fascinated with history and ancient cultures. She's a highly educated and respected anthropologist, and a well trained Starfleet officer, yet when she meets Khan, much of that well constructed, civilized veneer seems to fall away from her. McGivers not only falls in love with Khan—if you can call a severe, even quickie psycho crush love—but she helps to plot the hijacking of the Enterprise and betray her Captain and Starfleet crewmates.

Submission and domination of the libido fueled sexual variety—a kind of sci-fi *Fifty Shades of Grey*—surrounds the interpersonal dynamic of Khan and McGivers. When she hesitates on doing some task for him—being more cerebral deliberative than emotional and obedient about it—Khan gets almost violent with her and pushes her roughly to the ground.

Surprisingly, or maybe not, this kind of rough treatment seems to stimulate and attract McGivers to Khan all the more, and ultimately she allies herself with him and his group.

Comparing Montalban's Khan to Cumberbatch's Khan may be ultimately unfair; after all, nearly all of *Star Trek* fandom recognize Montalban Khan as the most powerfully fascinating villain from the classic Kirk helmed era. It's a wonder that as talented an actor as Cumberbatch agreed to the role, considering the irresistible creative shadow it casts lovingly over Roddenberry's sci-fi landscape. However, Abrams' creative team, in a real sense, castrated the character to such a degree that the Khan we knew is long gone.

Khaaaaaaaan! Gooooooone!

When forced to compare the two iconic Khans, we see a romantic, dashing, even passionate man in the original interpretation of the character, to Cumberbatch's serviceable version. The British actor brings a kind of bitter, vengeful or even petty spirit to his Khan. True, he didn't have the luxury of building the character from so strong a base as the story in *Space Seed*, and the character has been turned from a despotic, privileged ruler to something like a sad science experiment gone awry. It's easy to see why a woman like McGivers would be attracted to TOS's Khan, while the Khan we meet in *ST:ID* seems like he'd never need a woman—nor any romantic partner. He's too intent on playing vigilante—righting the wrongs of his slighted clan and playing terrorist, with no time for any romance indulgence—self serving or not.

In Kirk and Khan's relation dynamic there is also a sense of watching a dance; that of engaging the dominant and submissive sides of ourselves. Here, the stronger man who will not submit to the weaker, or the elder dominant to the younger. Khan, in his own life and through genetic manipulation, has lived nearly several lifetimes over the youthful Kirk. The problem with one submitting to the more dominant is that the two men are too well matched.

Though Khan may be far stronger physically, complete with a higher genetically boosted IQ, Kirk's brave, rebellious Starship commander recklessness appears to balance out the equation in the match up. By the time we get to see them go head to head in *STII:WOK*, it's a royal battle of steel wills—with one man so enraged over the death of his wife—Khan eventually married his love McGivers—he lets his emotions get the better of him when trying to dominate Admiral Kirk, which tasks him so much.

This Side Of Paradise
Sexual Situation: Rekindled Romance
StarDate: None Provided

> *Omicron Ceti III, a planet where a Federation colony had been established years before, is being showered by Berthold Rays. The radiation is lethal after several weeks of exposure, so when no word is heard from the colonists, Enterprise is dispatched on a recovery expedition. Startled to find the Federation colony not only alive and well, but prospering, Kirk and crew survey the site. However, after Spock reunites with a human woman, the usually non-emotional Vulcan suddenly starts expressing passionate feelings of love, joy, and even anger.*

Ever been so caught up in a love affair, so overwhelmed by the strong romantic feelings you have for another person, that you find it hard—or even scary—to tell them you love them? Maybe it's more of an insecurity or even fear of a possible rejection of our romantic honesty which so paralyzes our declaration of love. *Will they feel the same as I do? Will they laugh at me or tell me to go piss off?*

For the alien human hybrid Spock, things are always more complicated in the love life department. It's certainly not that a Vulcan is forbidden by their ancient culture to interact or even mate with other humanoid species. Spock is living example of such acceptance, as his mother, Amanda (Jane Wyatt) hails from Earth. His father, Sarek (Mark Lenard), an important Vulcan ambassador, married his human partner from which Spock was successfully created. Despite his mixed racial lineage, Spock carries himself as a full Vulcan male, capable of fully restraining all of his emotional output. When he's infected with the bizarre plant spores of Omicron Ceti III, Spock's emotional guard is drastically lowered and then, it's completely shattered.

Actress Jill Ireland (*Death Wish II*) plays Leila Kalomi, a beautiful human scientist from the colony, whose romantic past with Enterprise's first officer was one of physical, emotional and sexual frustration on her part. She's responsible for infecting her former flame Spock with the emotional liberating spores. And because of Ireland's excellent performance, we not only relate to her plight, but fairly cheer on her self centered actions. How fairytale convenient would it be if we could simply expose the one we love to a thing to free up their buried or conflicted emotions, turning an unrequited love affair into something mutually satisfying for both people.

Spock's emotions, and apparently even his physical appetites, have been liberated by the spores. He's a Vulcan who needs to mate—or is forced to mate—once every seven years. But the spores seem now to have erased any need for a strict timeline. He's kissing and snuggling at every opportunity, as if he and Leila are frolicking on a newlywed honeymoon. It's all blissful, even storybook romance textured—that is until Kirk himself is infected with the sex spouting spores.

Captain James T. Kirk may behave as a luscious Lothario of the cosmos, a veritable Tiger Woods or Arnold Schwarzenegger of the spaceways, a babe stashed away in every starbase, but, he has made no time for either a wife nor children—that we know of anyway, since the revelation of David Marcus was years away. He lives as if he wants as much physical love and sexual gratification as he can find, but not to cultivate the mature commitment nor responsibility when it comes to adult romance.

Could Kirk have a string of unwed baby mamas spread across a few star sectors, loaded down with a bunch of his star kids? It's indeed possible. That, however, would take a whole book in itself to properly explore.

When Kirk is spore injected, he nearly quits Starfleet to join the blissful band of merry men and women who've decided to drop out and become neo hippies (real flower children?) and live organically as vivacious vegetarians and whatnot on the paradisiacal Omicron Ceti III. At the last minute, deep and pestering thoughts of abandoning his career, of his starship commander legacy withering away, grab hold of him and get the better of him. He shakes off the spores' narcotic, valium-like influence. Kirk discovers powerful anger and raging emotions are like castor oil to the little bliss boosting buggers.

Since Kirk can't face giving up the majestic seat of Starfleet's flagship space faring vessel for a simple, basic life of healing love and recuperative joy, he must ruin things for everyone else—most specifically his friend and first Officer Spock. It's no secret that over the years these two men have fallen deeply in love with each other. Their sci-fi bromance is legendary. Maybe, above all, Kirk simply can't deal with the fact that his beloved Spock has now chosen another significant other over himself. Leila has now successfully taken Spock, something nothing else could ever do. She will take Kirk's place. The only thing which will bring him back is to break the sex spell of the libido liberating spores.

When Kirk attacks his Vulcan friend, it's a wholly, brutally emotional, even heart rending scene. He doesn't hit Spock physically, but unloads a withering verbal cavalcade, a mental body bashing of the most hurtful insults he can muster. Mostly, he attacks Spock as a 'half breed'—not fit to have sex with a human female. Spock weathers the verbal assault at first, and then caves in as he attempts to cave in his Captain's screaming skull. Kirk manages – doesn't he always—to keep from being murdered, and the tale ends with a crew snatched from paradise by the cold, cruel hand of their committed lives of Starfleet duty.

The City On The Edge Of Forever
Sexual Situation: Romantic Sacrifice
StarDate: No Stardate

While orbiting a planet which is home to a living time machine called The Guardian of Forever, the Enterprise is struck by a series of energy ribbons—or time energy ripples—emanating from the temporal entity. After the highly dynamic spatial and temporal vibrations cause Dr. McCoy to accidentally inject himself with a highly potent stimulant, he goes temporarily insane, and uses the Guardian to time travel back into Earth's past. Now, Kirk and Spock must travel through time and chase after Bones to prevent him from saving a life—before all of their known reality is changed for all of eternity.

Joan Collins is an actress with two iconic roles to her Hollywood credit. As ever scheming and bitchy—she more than helped to create the primetime bitch as we now know it—Alexis Carrington on nighttime soap opera *Dynasty*, Collins became known to all of the TV world as a ruthless, yet endlessly fascinating wealthy woman of immense power and influence. It is this character who engaged in the tortuous, yet entertaining manipulation of everyone around her. She was also one half of the hair pulling and wrestling dame duo, who took the girl fight concept to a whole new level. Opposite her favorite sparring partner, Linda Evans (*The Big Valley*), as Crystal Carrington, Collins spent many years sketching out a vibrant and indelible Hollywood mark on American pop culture.

As the well meaning—but dangerous to society's freedom and future—Edith Keeler, Collins spent about a week creating the unforgettable social worker for whom Captain Kirk falls madly in love with, but must abandon for a greater good. That in some ways Keeler is now the better known and remembered character, at least in the countries which embrace *Star Trek* more than *Dynasty*, is a credit to both *Trek*'s lasting power and Joan Collins' talent as an actress.

There is no other original series episode—nor in any of the spin-off shows—which so exemplifies the classical, romantic notion of a love which was meant to be, or even a love at first sight. Kirk and Spock don't have much time to locate McCoy and properly solve the mystery of why their civilization—*back to the future*—has been fully eroded or outright erased forever. Sure, it may arguably be seen as a convenient plot point to have Kirk swoon over Edith Keeler so relatively quickly, but William Shatner rises to the occasion of writer Harlan Ellison's famous script, and the pairing of the two actors makes for a truly unforgettable adventure.

Maybe it's because of what's riding on the outcome; the mountainous high stakes—all of the Federation's world building work, its citizens (not to mention countless other alien societies' influential connections and permutations) and very existence hangs in the balance, if Ms. Keeler is allowed to live and continue her mission of peace encouraging work. The suggested alternate timeline or historical timeline of the Axis Powers and Nazi regime snuffing out the Allies, Americans and Europeans is also compelling.

But, ultimately, it seems to go back to a simple and elegant love story. James T. Kirk falls in love with Edith Keeler—their titles and motivations don't really matter much in the end. A man and a woman come together, but are forbidden to fully consummate their blossoming love because of what it will mean to the entire world.

And then we have the plight of Bones—Dr. McCoy.

Dr. Leonard 'Bones' McCoy, the Southern gentleman and ship's physician, has had his share of romantic liaisons, but next to his commanding officer, he may appear almost a celibate monk. In this outing, because of his accidental overdose of the super stimulant McCoy was administering to Sulu, Bones is in no shape for romance—good, bad or otherwise. However, by the time he gets to Edith Keeler's charity soup kitchen, McCoy is healing and on the mend, and he's definitely looking at the committed social worker in a warm light. It nearly becomes a love triangle, but Bones never has time to woo the pretty social worker.

In the penultimate scene, as Kirk tenderly restrains his good friend McCoy from saving his new found savior from her death, it speaks to us as one of the most difficult and moving moments in all of the program's many installments. As Spock solemnly intones "He knows, Doctor. He knows," Kirk realizes he's allowed the woman he loves to expire before his grieving eyes. For McCoy, there may have been real potential denied. There could have been a seed of hope which he could have begun to nurture similar romantic feelings for the magnetic Edith Keeler. Finally, in her necessary death, both men are forever denied that winsome chance.

It isn't any wonder when Kirk says "Let's get the hell out of here," as he and his dazed crewmen return to their space faring home—the restored Starship Enterprise.

Amok Time

Sexual Situation: *Sexual Rage & Frenzy, Arranged Marriage*
StarDate: 3372.7

Starship Enterprise's science officer isn't doing so well lately. As a Vulcan, Spock must mate every seven years. It's his time now, and if he doesn't go back to his planet—like a salmon directed to spawn—he may not survive the ordeal for much longer. After getting special permission from Starfleet Command to ferry Spock back home, Kirk and McCoy are shocked to find he has a 'wife' waiting for him. T'Pring is beautiful, enigmatic, calculating and above all, she'll do anything to attain her highly logical and thoroughly ruthless goals.

Planet Vulcan is a UFP (United Federation of Planets) world full of stirring contrasts. It's an arid, desert planet, hot and unforgiving, yet its logic worshipping populace always maintain a cool, calm and collected exterior. But it wasn't always so orderly.

In ancient times, the Vulcans were so full of unbridled emotion and boiling over with unchecked rage, it nearly wiped out the entire race. To quell such destructive passions, the Vulcans adopted complete control over their volcanic emotions and pursued complex reasoning and logic to help to order their chaotic lives. One of the most sweeping and basic drives, sexuality, comes under this monastic-like control of unifying primal body with a gymnastic-like mind.

Amid McCoy's medical ministrations of the ailing (clinically horny) Spock, Nurse Chapel steps in and tries to help by using her own remedy. She attempts to soothe the fiery Vulcan she pines for so romantically with a steaming bowl of plomeek soup—undoubtedly it's something like Vulcan chicken soup, only more bland tasting. When the soup and tray she delivers it on is sent crashing into a corridor wall at warp speed, it's clear Spock really needs some intense sexual healing. So Marvin Gaye is ramped up loudly in the crew's mind and the grand starship warps off to Vulcan to return the spawning Spock home to roost.

Kirk and McCoy beam down with the ever heavy breathing Spock to meet with the Vulcan dignitary presiding over the sexual fulfillment and mating ritual associated with the Vulcan pon farr. T'Pau, an elderly (even, it appears, by Vulcan long lived standards) Vulcan holds court over the ancient martial arts contest. This will be no TV reality-like horseplay—ala *The Dating Game* or *Love Connection*. Spock isn't going to behave like an alien version of *The Bachelor*. These stakes are slightly higher than scoring a date or winning a new car or trip to the Bahamas—try love, life and certain death.

Although a good portion of the episode plays like a Roman gladiatorial contest, or these days, like a weapons allowed MMA or UFC fight, the underlying sexual tension surrounding the whole affair is the far more interesting dynamic of the powerful story. While Kirk and McCoy listen to T'Pau officiate and T'Pring discuss the match rules and dynamics of the ritual, Spock stands aside and apart from the gathering. He's seething with restrained sexual energy—his hands clasped in a tight, prayer-like configuration, his eyes rolling and lolling back into his head. He looks nearly possessed—like Linda Blair's demonic charged Regan in *The Exorcist*.

When Kirk agrees to become Spock's opponent, he can't imagine his friend and first officer ever taking the whole thing so seriously that he'd almost get his head bashed in or be choked to death. Wasn't our good Captain paying attention? Didn't he hear McCoy's medical assessment of Spock's condition? This Kirk is way too trusting, or maybe just a little slow from the withering Vulcan heat. But I guess that's also what deep friendship encourages and even demands of one.

Finally, of course, Kirk is also put at ease by the Vulcan's peerless training and sterling background. Spock is a highly trained Starfleet officer—he would never seek to truly harm another Starfleet comrade, even in the thick cloud of a sexually frustrated rage.

Or would he? Lust does strange things to a man.

T'Pring is a brazenly resourceful woman. She uses the apparent antiquated Vulcan social system to her full advantage. She knows that arranged marriage is still practiced and important to Vulcans, yet by pitting Kirk against his first officer, she knows that no matter the outcome, she should come up on top of the nasty heap.

Ultimately, though a true TOS classic, and one of the most robust expressions of *Star Trek Sex*, it does seem just a tad backwards that the highly progressive Vulcans, full of their high tech science and high minded philosophy, are still subject and bound by such ancient gender roles and old school rules. But it's supremely fun seeing Spock gleefully take the hot air out of the superior T'Pring at the close of the rollicking tale.

We can almost hear Spock say, "Indeed. Fascinating. That was most savagely logical, bitch."

Who Mourns For Adonais?
Sexual Situation: God & Mortal Romance
StarDate: 3468.1

> *Starship Enterprise has encountered many strange new worlds and new lifeforms. The Starfleet crew under command of Captain James T. Kirk rallied against crazy Klingons, ruthless Romulans and dealt effectively with that fuzzy scourge—determined to keep their space vessel purring pest free—Tribbles. But now to come face to face with an honest to goodness Greek God of days gone by? When Apollo grabs hold of Kirk's crew, both literally and figuratively, it's soon clear that no matter the true identity of the entity, his powers are awesome and his will absolute.*

Greek mythology fascinates, educates and entertains us all. Scripture-like in its complex documentation and scope, yet still flexible and organic enough to withstand repeated retellings slightly or even vastly different in details, the epic tales of Zeus, Hera, Aphrodite and Apollo continue to charm the world of mortal man. Big Hollywood movies like *Clash of the Titans* and *Immortals* rake in huge, global box office gold. Superman? Hercules with a cape. The Flash? Hermes in red tights. Comic book heroes, in the most basic of ways, delight as modern versions of godly exploits.

The crew of Constitution class Starship Enterprise aren't new to the god gotcha game. Gary Mitchell and Charlie Evans both displayed irresistible godlike powers. Mitchell even fancied himself one, after a fashion, but he was effectively dispatched by his mortal friend and Enterprise commander. Charlie, much like Trelane in *Squire of Gothos*, is the product or beneficiary of alien abilities and super advanced tech. What of an awesome being who appears to all as a Greek God and behaves accordingly?

Apollo (Michael Forest) is unabashedly the real deal—at least in his own mind and following his own self important narrative. He makes no apologies for thundering around—at one point growing himself to 50 feet tall or so—in a Greek style costume, and thunderously reading the cosmic riot act to Enterprise's mortals—Captain Kirk, Spock, Scotty and Chekov. He refuses to compromise or peel back the curtain on his impressive magic show. For all intents and purpose, the ultra modern men and women of Starfleet—light years away from planet Earth, and centuries removed from the mist shrouded classicism of Ancient Greece—must now pay homage, tribute and obey an all powerful being who claims to be an Earth god.

Where's *Roseanne* when you need her? Domestic Goddess meets a real Greek God.

There's one person however, whom Apollo doesn't so much want a primal and worshipful obeisance, as the storybook romance his persona simply demands from any human being who encounters him and his mythical grandeur. In one Enterprise crewmember, Lt. Carolyn Palamas, Apollo appears completely enthralled. Played by the beautiful actress Leslie Parrish, the self promoting Greek god of light and music is so romantically taken with the blonde bombshell that in his pursuit of her, he considers, even promises, making her into her equal. He tells her, "You will know what it is to be a Goddess."

Like the too bright eyed Gary Mitchell, like the bratty adolescent Charlie Evans, and like the prancing, dancing trickster alien child Trelane of Gothos, these godlike guys always are in need of a complimentary female force: the stabilizing feminine yin to their conquering masculine yang. They immediately seek out and find a female counterpart—their queen. Could Apollo with his nifty magic bag of tricks transform Lt. Palamas into his feminine, super powered equal? Perhaps. But even if he couldn't, it's clear he'll be content to have her by his side as his love and a fellow ruler over her human Starfleet crew.

Though flattered by his godly attention, Palamas won't allow herself to be crowned nor invite the crew to attend her royal coronation so easily. She's not willing to give up her self or compromise her identity like Marla McGivers, nor is she concerned about the disparity in age like Yeoman Rand putting off Charlie—though if Apollo really is the Greek God version from Earth, that's some vast age difference, indeed!

And then there's our favorite engineer, Scotty. *Aye. Aye.*

At times, because of Scotty's romantic admiration for Carolyn Palamas, the episode plays like a lopsided love triangle. In the opening scene, Kirk and Bones discuss Scotty's growing admiration for Palamas and how he's convinced himself he's the right man for her, but is she convinced of the same? It's the kind of small talk many friends or coworkers would have with each other, but it foreshadows things to come in the romance department for the hyperactive Scotsman.

The Chief Engineer of Enterprise simply can't compete on the same playing field as a cosmic powered entity like Apollo, but this doesn't dissuade him from actually trying—nor from backing down when Apollo gets too frisky and friendly with Carolyn. Scotty nearly pays with his life for daring to challenge a god. Carolyn must not only challenge a god herself, but hurt and even lie to him. Ultimately, her love for Apollo can't get in the way of her sworn duty to her Starship, crew and Captain. It is that sense of committed duty and personal obligation which strongly sets apart the Starfleet crew we all admire so much.

Mirror, Mirror
Sexual Situation: Attempted rape
StarDate: Unknown

After Captain Kirk and an away team beam back to Enterprise from dilithium mining negotiations on a planet, things on the starship have apparently changed. Instead of a peace loving Vulcan first officer guiding an obedient, scrupulous crew, they find a steely eyed, even cruel Spock surrounded by a crew scheming for promotions. This Enterprise crew will stop at nothing—not even assassination—to get ahead. Welcome to an alternative or parallel universe, where Kirk's crew must find a way back to their own Enterprise, before these ruthless, predatory counterparts stop or even kill them.

Mirror, mirror on the wall, who's the most cunning one of them all?
The self serving crew of the ISS Enterprise wouldn't necessarily care about cosmetic beauty, but they'd definitely wish to know who the most clever and cunning competitor among them was so they could take them out permanently. Like *Star Trek* colliding with the ruthless HBO crime

family *The Sopranos*, the Spock, Chekov and Sulu we meet in this parallel universe, would do Tony and his crew proud in executing hits and operating under the rules of who can pay the highest protection price or suffer fatal consequences.

Among all of this chaotic anarchy slinks the beautiful Lt. Marlena Moreau.

Marlena is certainly a sultry one, and, after all, she is the *Captain's Woman*. His own personal sexual partner? Is she a kind of classy prostitute or pro sex therapist rolled up into one? Whatever her full backstory, or her official capacity is, one thing is crystal clear: She's got the Captain's back by being privy to the dreaded Tantalus Field. Marlena knows how to operate this powerful offensive device and she's not afraid to use the awesome weapon.

When our more civilized Kirk encounters her, he knows that his parallel baddie self must rely on Lt. Moreau for much in his highly successful career. And Marlena knows just how important she is to the command structure of the darkly commanded starship. The Captain's Woman isn't merely a title—it's a sense of entitlement earned by assisting her lover and leader in all the things to contribute to his ascendancy through the ranks of the ISS—Imperial Star Ship.

Finally, as Kirk, Scotty, McCoy and Uhura are embroiled in a fight with the scarred and forever evilly grinning Sulu, and his loyal security goons, Marlena Moreau proves she really does live up to the title of Captain's Woman. Utilizing the irresistible offensive powers of the Tantalus Field, she zaps the goons away into its otherworldly or interdimensional version of the cornfield. Even the predacious Sulu from this pitiless dimension is no match for the eternally testosterone driven, Karate chopping Kirk, who makes short work of his mirror helmsman. They make off to the transporter room to get ferried back to the proper universe version for themselves. The exotic and enigmatic Lt. Moreau, however, awaits them. She's armed with a phaser and she has a high price for her assistance.

She demands to be taken back with them to the more civilized universe. Imagine—as clever, conniving and ruthless a woman as the mirror Marlena Moreau let loose in our universe? Kim Kardashian wouldn't have to worry about her reality show anymore, she'd be too busy looking over her shoulder at Miss Moreau.

Moreau won't bargain with Kirk, so Uhura must disarm her of her phaser. The Van Dyke bearded Spock comes in just in time to have our

Kirk lecture him on the illogic of the social system he helps maintain. Spock, in any time or dimension, is always logical and he's convinced the Kirk from another universe is right. He sends our people home. And that's that—well, mostly.

On the bridge, Kirk encounters a new member of his crew—a Lieutenant Moreau—the mirror counterpart of the Captain's Woman from where he just escaped. Leave it to Kirk to set his sex hungry eyes upon her and he will undoubtedly try to turn her into one of his many conquests. Will she be as duplicitous and self serving as her mirror alternate? Maybe Kirk thinks he can handle her if that's the challenging case.

Or maybe, that's just what our Kirk thinks will be fun in discovering for himself.

The Apple
Sexual Situation: Arranged Romantic Unions—Sexual Repression
StarDate: 3715.3

> *When Enterprise pays a visit to Gamma Trianguli VI, the world's lush foliage appears to confirm to the away team that the place beckons as a wondrous paradise. Not so fast though, because upon closer inspection, a paradise isn't normally known for exploding rocks or flowers which spray forth poisonous spores. The worst part of it all? The planet's inhabitants are gentle, almost childlike humanoids who are fully controlled by a smoke spewing 'Dragon God'—who oversees and lords over all the minutiae in their simplistic lives—including their sexual partners, or lack thereof.*

What is love?

Let's also ask—What is paradise? All you can eat. Beautiful weather. Lush, tropical foliage. Loads of hot people scantily dressed around you. Sounds like your definition of paradise?

What's the catch? You can't date who you want to date. Nobody knows what kissing is – let alone getting to those all important bases. And you know you're really in trouble when those all around you question what love is and firmly proclaim that '*the holding and the touching*' is forbidden.

Did your parents forbid you to date someone? Even worse, or perhaps going truly old school, did they ever suggest or even arrange for a date or rendezvous with a potential date or mate? For the residents of

Gamma Trianguli VI, that silly, papier-mâché chic Dragon God, Vaal, plays ruler, farmer and even matchmaker—or not.

Today, gay, lesbian, transgender and even some interracial or interfaith couples still have a hard time being demonstrative in public with their romances or justifying their love to the more closed minded and intractable thinking among us. Is Vaal a sci-fi symbol of a repressive government like the present Russian one, where President Vladimir Putin seems to discourage—or at the very least—look down upon gay individuals as having fewer rights?

Instead of another 'love and leave 'em' or maybe even 'reassign 'em to another starship' Kirk love tale, we are treated to the Russian Valentino of sorts, Ensign Chekov, who's here front and center in the romance department. Apparently Chekov's Beatle-esque haircut has successfully snared one of his fellow Enterprise crew to his charms. Yeoman Martha Landon, played by the gorgeous Celeste Yarnall—a feature film co-star of Elvis Presley—is Chekov's current squeeze. The planet they are working on for their current mission seems more than conducive to nurturing the two's blossoming starship based love fest. Leave it to our ever optimistic Bones to find the disruptive fly in the pastoral ointment.

"This isn't life! This is stagnation!" says Dr. McCoy deftly describing the social system on the planet, as he verbally spars with Spock over how there's been no real change in the humanoids on the planet in over ten thousand years. Spock confidently fires back that "... these people are healthy and they are happy. Whatever you choose to call it, this system works."

And then the naturally horny Chekov and Landon start to make out in front of the natives.

Those two randy kids and their lusty canoodling send powerful ripples of chaotic change into the happy nest of Vaal's tribe. Soon, the once gentle and inviting aliens—dripping with heavy eye make-up—start to plot to kill the Enterprise party by bashing in their little human heads with sticks. *Why?* Because Vaal wills it. Is this the over protective safe guarding of a security system gone out of control? Or maybe it's simply more inconveniently biological. Is this what happens when sexual repression eats away at the normal and healthy procreating fabric of a society? Does it drive people to cold blooded murder?

We're all aware of how damaging to anyone's good health—at any adult age—the lack of sexual partners or a sexual outlet can be. Now the artificial intelligent high school play looking prop seeks to compound things by teaching the once innocents to cave in another's head. No sex, nor physical intimacy allowed, but brutal, cold blooded murder encouraged? Thanks, Vaal.

Paradise lost indeed.

Fun aside: Engineer humor. When Mr. Scott learns the Enterprise transporter system has been compromised, he tells Kirk, "We can't beam up a fly!" Is Scotty—that old Scottish sassmaster—being funny when he makes a reference, however innocent, to beaming up a housefly? All well educated sci-fi lovers know the classic science fiction horror movie, *The Fly*, dealt with the transportation screw up which mated man and fly. Is Scotty invoking that image—or is it merely a coincidence?

Metamorphosis
Sexual Situation: Non-corporeal sex & love, three way love making, threesomes
StarDate: 3219.8

> *While ferrying a gravely ill diplomat to Enterprise for medical treatment, a shuttlecraft with Kirk, Spock and McCoy aboard encounters a blob of sparkling energy which downs the shuttle in one piece onto a neighboring planet. The castaways soon meet Zephram Cochrane, legendary inventor of the fabled warp drive no less, who was marooned here over a century before. He tells them they'll never leave the world, because the energy blob which forced them down is sentient. It will likely keep them stranded forever.*

Unrequited love. It can be the heart aching curse of a whole lifetime. How can one who pines for the love of another get along each day or fully exist without the intense pain or even daily torture if their romantic longing isn't fulfilled?

For the Earth spawned human being Zephram Cochrane, it's a matter of an alien love story which isn't exactly being written out or performed to his liking or satisfaction. He's been marooned far from home and he's the object of desire of a creature so powerful and incomprehensible that it can rejuvenate—deage him so that his true age of 225 years or so fades away. He's now for all the world a youthful thirty five year old man. But how can a vital human male return the carnal love of an incorporeal thing—a creature of pulsating energy? Can he sublimate his own physical and mental needs and adapt to such a relationship? Could anyone do so? Could you?

The arrival of the human diplomat, Nancy Hedford, both complicates matters and simplifies them at the same time. She's terribly ill—but that basic human physiology of taking ill is what the Companion is more than capable of treating and healing. When it does so, and when it merges into Nancy to become a hybrid being, it can now relate to Cochrane on a human, physical level.

However, the Companion has made a sacrifice in becoming human by merging with Nancy. It can no longer utilize its miraculous energies to rejuvenate and prolong human life. It means that it will not only itself run the course of a normal human lifespan, but now Cochrane's life clock will no longer be stalled on pause. They will both grow older together and finally pass away one day. Love traded in for a certain promise of death.

Did the Companion shortchange its own existence by becoming human? Or was the final decision which Zephram Cochrane made, to stay with the Nancy Companion hybrid, the only proper one to make? After all, all of his family and friends are now surely long gone. He couldn't celebrate their lives, nor mourn their deaths. He's a man completely out of time, and he made the effort to leave the planet Earth centuries earlier anyway. But still, there are lingering questions about the solution to the Companion-Nancy-Cochrane threesome.

If the Companion could meld and merge so easily with a human being, why didn't it just do so to Cochrane in the first place? It would still perhaps die as a normal human after a normal lifespan, but it would be merged with its love until they both expired. The experience of being so close with the one you love sounds like it would be the ultimate relationship, but of course, it's possible that Cochrane may have freaked out or objected to such a new kind of life for himself. And there would have been no turning back.

In the end, Zephram Cochrane, Nancy and the Companion can share something unique—as they are embarking on the ultimate in a romantic and spiritual threesome. Their three way relationship may be unorthodox, even bizarre, but it appears that it will work perfectly well for them.

The next time you're offered to partake in a romantic threesome, think about Zephram Cochrane, Nancy and the wondrous Companion.

Wolf In The Fold
Sexual Situation: Psychosexual Serial Killer
StarDate: 3614.9

> *Scotty a pathological serial killer? Jack The Ripper resurrected and roaming the streets once more prowling for innocent prey? The Enterprise computer spouting death threats and displaying the fiery gateways to hell itself? It seems that most anything—dread, nightmarish and murderous—can happen on the exotic planet of Argelius II. After Chief Engineer Montgomery Scott is found next to a corpse and holding the murder weapon, it's a journey into the mind of a madness which has existed and slaughtered scores of victims for untold ages.*

Scotty isn't exactly known for his reputation as a ladies' man of Starfleet. And considering his romantic track record with dating hopefuls like Lt. Carolyn Palamas—from *Who Mourns For Adonais?*—the Chief Engineer of Starship Enterprise may as well spend even more quality time in the ship's engine room than trolling the lounges for companionship. At least he's not like that other engineer. You know, the one who spends far too much time in a holodeck, but hey, that's another *generation*—to each his own.

When Scotty takes Kara, the Argelian belly dancer for a walk, there's nothing particularly weird about it, but we may not be focused on the foggy streets and alleys of the town. Thick fog is always an ominous sign of impending trouble. What's more troubling is Dr. McCoy's professional medical assessment of Scott's 'level of resentment' towards women—which could lead to violence or even murder. That Bones is not a dedicated psychiatrist may not matter so much (Where's Counselor Troi when you need her?), since all physicians must be versed somewhat in the study of human psychology. Still, it seems a bit of a leap to diagnose Scotty as being dangerous to women—because of his recent physical altercation with a woman.

Scotty received a mild concussion from the incident, yet seems fine when the men are partying in the opening teaser. Today, we are armed with conclusive and damning medical evidence about concussions. We know when pro athletes and sports figures—especially NFL players—suffer bad concussions over time, devastating mental and neurological consequences from these injuries can arise. Massive financial class action suits have been filed against sports team owners, charging that players not only became physically violent to wives, girlfriends and other family members, but many became suicidal and took their own lives.

What's most interesting in a twisted, pathological sexuality way about the creation of this episode is the writer—Robert Bloch. Bloch is the author who wrote the novel *Psycho*—the book which was used as the basis for Alfred Hitchcock's 1960 classic tale of cinema terror. Any fan of the cinematic master of suspense will delight in this Hollywood connection.

Is Scotty really Norman Bates? At the end of *Wolf In The Fold*, we learn that an incorporeal entity named Redjac or Beratis—it has assumed many guises and has gone by many infamous names throughout the galaxy and the ages—is truly responsible for all the grisly murders, but McCoy's psychological summation of Scotty is truly damning.

Indeed, Norman Bates, based upon the real life serial killer Ed Gein, has resentment towards women. In Hitchcock's unforgettable film, whenever Norman gets sexually aroused around a beautiful girl, he must do away with those feelings. He must kill her to satisfy a female side of his own self—his own deceased mother, whom he himself murdered years earlier. Is Scotty's murder rampage—fueled on by the alien entity—his *Star Trek* tribute to his own novel? Despite the tale's close of the murdering creature being dispatched, this episode seems to forever tar Montgomery Scott as a man who has problems relating to the gals around him.

He may even be forever nicknamed Norman by his starship compatriots.

The Trouble With Tribbles
Sexual Situation: Born pregnant species
StarDate: 4523.3

Deep Space Station K7 sounds out an urgent distress call. It seems a security detail is needed to guard the safe passage of a shipment of grain making its way to Sherman's Planet—a world which is being disputed over by the Klingon Empire and the Federation. All of it seems a necessary, yet boring duty to Kirk and his crew; that is until Cyrano Jones shows up. Jones is a trader of just about everything; in particular he boasts the most curious fuzzy pet— a Tribble. These little furballs appear perfectly harmless at first,

until they begin procreating wildly and consuming the grain En-
terprise is here to protect.

Remember, all of you Furby fans, Tribbles were here first!

It should be noted that Tribbles are not nearly as annoying as Furbys. That said, this episode is basically a tale of an exotic and adorable pet run dangerously amok. The episode plays like a fun and bouncy romp, but aside from yet another outing with Klingons as the weekly villain, the main draw and staying power here is the now legendary Tribble. Even those who don't know a phaser from a laser, or why Spock's ears are so darned pointy (actually, does anybody know *why*?), have probably heard of or may even own a prop replica or a toy Tribble. Like super obese lint balls or fluffy cotton balls on steroids, the furry, purring things are firmly entrenched in our pop culture tapestry.

How could any one of us reject a small, fuzzy purring ball of love? This must be the greatest tactical advantage the seemingly innocuous Tribble has over us. Even the smallest, or most self sufficient of pets need some level of care and responsibility, but Tribbles seem to be able to take care of themselves quite nicely. Left alone to their own rapacious devices, they not only live long and prosper—but they multiply, and multiply and multiply...

Tribbles are incredibly efficient at procreation. Fantastic or tire-less lovers? No. It's something much simpler, even elegant. They're born pregnant. As Dr. McCoy tells Kirk, "Almost fifty percent of the creature's metabolism is geared for reproduction." To which Kirk answers, "Well, Bones, all I can suggest is—you open up a maternity ward."

As the fuzzy, cosmic dust bunnies keep on multiplying way out of control, they are seemingly unaware of how dangerous such unchecked population growth can be to the welfare and longevity of a species. When the grain shipment of quadrotriticale is found poisoned and starts killing the always famished little beasties, it seems to act like a natural predator to stem the ever ballooning numbers.

Could creatures born pregnant be helpful in scientific, medical re-search or even tactical ways? Say as a more efficient way to deliver a tacti-cal measure in a defensive fashion or even an offensive way to an enemy in warfare? Imagine tactical drones made up of Tribble-like creatures not needing replenishment in the traditional way—but whose ranks are al-ways swelled back up through their own procreation. Imagine: Wave after wave of pregnant Tribbles—being poured over an enemy troop line as their puffy ranks swelled ever more pregnant and maternity offensive in some advanced Starfleet tech way.

At the end, when Scotty beams the load of fuzzy beasties over and onto the Klingon ship and proudly announces, "Where they'll be no Tribble at all!", we are assured that Captain James T. Kirk's crew do their demanding jobs efficiently, albeit with a decidedly sadistic streak. Will Starfleet use Tribbles as an offensive weapon against Klingons? Clearly, Scotty should act as consultant to help get that project off the ground, since he has expertise in utilizing Tribbles in such an advanced tactical capacity.

Live long and be born pregnant.

Assignment: Earth
Sexual Situation: Interspecies Love, Love Triangle & Sexual Shapeshifting
StarDate: None Provided

Who exactly is the mysterious Gary Seven? When Enterprise travels back in time to 1968 on a mission to conduct a little sociological research on the historical doings of the time, they encounter an enigmatic humanoid. Intercepting his transporter beam, Gary Seven is taken aboard the Starship and held in detention. He soon easily escapes, carrying with him a black cat named Isis, a 'pen' which can do more high tech magic than any tricorder, and his confidential mission. Seven has many toys at his disposal, but his befuddled secretary, Roberta Lincoln, may be the most unlikely of allies and prove far more valuable than any cool gadget in Seven's fascinating bag of tech tricks.

Star Trek, with the great offshoot success of *The Next Generation*, *Deep Space Nine*, *Voyager* and *Enterprise*, is well known for its popular spin-off TV shows. What isn't widely known by many fans is that one proposed spin-off show never made it to production, but was 'tested' as a backdoor pilot in this fun romp. Starring Robert Lansing as Gary Seven and Terri Garr (*Tootsie*) as the lovable, yet light headed Ms. Roberta Lincoln, *Assignment: Earth* could have become yet another classic Gene Roddenberry television series.

We'll never know if such a show would have been as well received as other later Roddenberry offerings like the syndicated programs *Earth: Final Conflict* or *Andromeda*, starring Kevin Sorbo of *Hercules: The Leg-*

endary Journeys fame. However, we can safely deduce from watching this episode that the well drawn characters would have been a hit with fans. The authentic chemistry between Lansing and Garr is certainly always in fine tune and welcome. Even if the show itself wasn't overly brimming with action and spectacular FX eye candy, these two actors display an easy and comfortable connection which viewers would have loved.

Close examination, however, reveals that the duo is, in fact, a trio.

Despite the brief pairing of the two and how little they know one another, it's clear to us that Seven and Lincoln could easily have had a fling or a 'thing' for one another. If such a romance ever kindled and blossomed fully—and we all know from examples like Sam and Diane from *Cheers*, that can be a dangerous road for a show to go down—there would have been another waiting patiently in the wings. This character, though alluring and seductive, would be a hard, even bestial opponent to face in the love game for Ms. Lincoln. For one thing, her rival for the love and affection of Gary Seven had four feet and sharp claws.

Isis appeared as an exotic cat and then as an even more exotic woman. She seemed to fill out both of these roles quite nicely. Her morphing from cat to woman and back again makes her something of a shape shifter—or at least one well versed in projecting a kind of ultra convincing illusion. The subtext between this feline companion and Gary Seven turns the exotic fare well into the steamy erotic.

We never do learn how exactly Isis does her stunning feline tricks. She's obviously an alien life form—or a human female who's learned a great deal more from those advanced aliens than Seven—who acts as Seven's companion, protector, and perhaps even his lover. Did the aliens who taught and trained Seven for his purpose also train Isis? Is she a kind of genetically modified life form, or one even grown and matured in a laboratory test tube? Maybe she's a kind of sexy Jem H'adar warrior or seductive Vorta?

Maybe the reason Isis takes the form of an onyx cat and bears the Egyptian Goddess' name is because these unknown aliens have a loyal allegiance or connection to the empires of Ancient Egypt. Are they simply emulating the look and terminology of Egyptian royalty—or like the alien super beings in the *StarGate* mythos, and Apollo from *Who Mourns For Adonais*, are they alien lifeforms who injected their own special and advanced cultures onto the primitive peoples of ancient Earth?

The Enterprise Incident
Sexual Situation: Seduction
StarDate: 5027.3

After Enterprise warps into the dangerous political space of The Neutral Zone, Kirk and Spock play dual versions of James Bond and Jason Bourne coordinating a top secret Starfleet intelligence mission. Spock must carefully navigate the tricky waters of being seduced by a sultry Romulan Commander. Meanwhile, Captain Kirk—after faking his death at Spock's Vulcan Death Grip dealing hands—poses as a Romulan to steal a cloaking device.

Kirk, James T. Kirk. I take my Romulan Ale shaken, not stirred.

Captain James Tiberius Kirk has often been compared to the British superspy James Bond for his shared lusty love of the ladies, and how easily the two dashing heroes seem to always win out at the end—no matter the great odds stacked against them. Here, he and First Officer Spock go J. Bond and J. Bourne for the high stakes sake of stealing a Romulan cloaking device.

Romulans, as the genetic cousins (and by far the rowdier chaps) to the peaceful Vulcans, are the intelligence challenge here, and as the episode's chief antagonist, we have the seductive Romulan Commander. She's a mature, responsible and centered woman—one who's apparently been around the cosmic block more than a few times. Spock too is no babe in the woods, but with magnetic actress Joanne Linville playing the Romulan leader, we get the sense Spock is challenged both by the mission's mechanics and also operating freely around such a powerfully erotic female.

We're again reminded of Spock's complex biology—the chronological structured love demands and libido leash of the Vulcan Pon Farr—or their time of mating. Spock looks as if he'd neatly throw that little inconvenient, biological ritual right out of the nearest airlock. Still, above all the dance of fluid flirting—authentic, spontaneous or for the intelligence mission's success at nurturing verisimilitude—we all know and believe Spock is eternally loyal. He's a company man through and through. Would he shirk his Starfleet duty and throw away a respectable career and reputation for a roll in the hay with this Romulan temptress? Even one attached with the promise of his own command in the Romulan fleet?

Like the sentient android Data's personal revelation to Captain Picard at the end of *Star Trek: First Contact*, there is a sense that things could have turned out much differently. Data revealed to his Captain that he was indeed tempted by the Borg Queen's offer to make him human—or at least to give him all the organic and human-like trappings of a real human being—skin, the promise of sexual stimulation and love making—etc. Spock, if only to be polite (though Vulcans aren't known for such human conventions) tells the Romulan Commander basically the same thing. He was indeed tempted by her offer—if only for a logically brief time.

Love—or sex—is never logical, Mr. Spock.

Is There In Truth No Beauty?
Sexual Situation: Romantic Jealousy, Love Triangle
StarDate: 5630.7

Can only the visually blind know what's truly universally beautiful? For the telepath Miranda Jones, her disability allows her to 'see' more so and more clearly than most sighted people will ever be able to view over several human lifetimes. Her problem is envy. She's jealous of all those with similar gifts who come in contact with Kollos—a Medusan ambassador. Medusans are fantastically accomplished psychics, making them mentally attractive, even beautiful. However, like the racial, mythical namesake, the impact of their physical and external appearance mentally obliterates all who look upon them.

Who sayes that fictions onely and false hair
Become a verse? Is there in truth no beauty?
Is all good structure in a winding stair?
May no lines passe, except they do their dutie
Not to a true, but painted chair?" -- Jordan by George Herbert

Miranda Jones (Diana Muldaur) is being devoured internally by an intense jealousy. She's so in love and completely obsessed with her employer—the famous Medusan ambassador, Kollos—that all who appear as a challenge to her position are perceived as a threat to be dealt with ruthlessly. Here, the threat to her place is a more powerful telepath—the First Officer of the Enterprise, Mr. Spock.

Vulcans are advanced psychic beings. With their powerful telepathic abilities, the Federation's logic lovers are able to span vast physical distances to feel the emotions of or even communicate with other beings, especially other Vulcans. The most powerful, and certainly one of the most useful psychic tools at their mental disposal, is the mind meld. By laying on the hands and establishing a psychic link with another's mind, the Vulcan can know the thoughts and feelings of another—Vulcan or not.

We've seen Spock mind meld with all sorts of humanoids and entities—and even a shambling rock creature in the bizarre Horta from *Devil In The Dark*. Here, Miranda Jones, after causing Spock to forget his protective visor and suffer psychological damage from gazing upon the Medusan, must engage in her own version of a mind meld with Spock to help repair the damage.

Imagine the magnified stress and performance anxiety one would feel if the entirety of a person's mental health welfare and future rested upon their competence in successfully reaching the now deranged core mind—to navigate carefully inside the damaged neurology of a living brain. Combine this with the resentment and insecurity Miranda Jones feels when she's around someone as strong as Spock. Now not only must she help him, but she must heal him and bring him back from the brink.

In the midst of it all is the pathetic instigator of the near destruction of both the starship Enterprise and, indirectly, the mental ruination of Spock: Lawrence Marvick. Marvick isn't just any old respected Starship designer and engineer. He's one of the primary designers of Kirk's majestic, warping glory—the Starship Enterprise itself.

Marvick acts as the dangerous fly in this chaotic ointment. He's the kind of pitiable man whose disruptive sexual desires and dalliances highly impact all those around him. Think of the scathing sex scandals of President Bill Clinton, Congressman Mark Sanford or Twitter Twit Twat Andrew Weiner—politicians who simply can't resist the sexual temptation of mixing their private life into the public arena, and subsequently embroil their constituency or even an entire country into a tawdry pleasure playpen.

For Lawrence Marvick, it's not political destruction as issue (wonder what Starfleet's version of Twitter is), but professional and even life threatening behavior. When Marvick goes to kills Kollos, we root for him to be caught or even done away with—since it's such a bloodthirsty and cold blooded act of murder. His jealousy of Kollos boils him into such a pulpy, psychotic mess it nearly destroys everyone.

Miranda Jones also allows jealousy to get the better of her, but in the final act, she makes things right by tossing aside her bruised feelings and saving Spock. It's a dual lesson in the potential destructive power of jealousy and how much it can damage multiple lives or even take them away.

A Private Little War

Sexual Situation: Sex/Love Potion, Aphrodisiac, Attempted Rape
StarDate: 4211.4

> *On Planet Neural, an intense war between primitive tribesmen natives is brewing. On the surface, it seems a straightforward enough fight, but it's really not the fairly armed and objective conflict that it appears. One of the sides is being supported by the Klingons, who are arming them with better weapons. If protecting the primitive natives against Klingons violating the prime directive isn't enough, Captain Kirk must deal with a smoldering sexy witch doctor who's managed to zap him with a kind of aphrodisiac/love potion which threatens to enslave his very soul.*

We know of hopeful types among us needing sexual assistance who seek out the use of aphrodisiacs—however ineffective or fictional they may be—and some claim that they even work. The remedies run the gamut of ingesting spices, herbs or even employing items such as charms. Foods like oysters or the ingesting of various mega-vitamins supposedly also promise to help boost the libido or make one a better, more energetic lover in the sack. Even modern pharmacy wonders like Viagra or Cialis can provide a male partner with enough drug backed stamina to fuel their tired tool for all night love making sessions.

What of the legendary love potion? Can sexual attraction or even true love be made to order with a pop of a pill or the imbibing of a drink? Is the magic of Cupid's Arrow merely waiting to be replicated synthetically in a test tube?

The native witch doctor or the Kahn-ut-tu on Neural is a sexy woman named Nona. Her knowledge and expertise with the planet's herbs enables her to heal the physical injury of the wounded—especially those who succumb to the deadly bite of the ferocious Mugato. The Mugato is a towering albino-like ape creature with spiny back and unicorn-like horn on its head. After it bites Kirk, he's going to require the proper medical attention, or he'll pay with his life.

Nona heals Kirk by mixing and mingling her own blood with his tainted own. They've become the ultimate blood brothers and according to the mythology of the hill people, Kirk has now become hers—in essence, he is her property. He'll not be able to say no to her regarding any request she may make of him.

Love potion extreme!

Nona isn't simply after Kirk as a man or even her slave; she wants much more. She's after the advanced weapon technology which he can provide—namely those marvelous little fire boxes, phasers. But despite the intense hold Nona has over him, Kirk won't give in to her demands and so she must steal what she's sought to charm him into giving her.

With the nifty little firebox in hand, Nona takes her prize to negotiate with the enemy villagers. She proclaims how wondrous is the object she holds up to them—how it will tip the balance of power in their favor, but they don't hear her. They don't care. The only thing they care about is violating her sexually. After repeated attempts at trying to rape her fail, Kirk and Nona's mate finally rush onto the scene to save her from the sexual predators, but it's too late. The rampaging villagers, furious over not being able to violate her, stab and kill her instead.

As her mate mourns her, McCoy retrieves the phaser from her dead hand and so ends the woman's life who tried to use sex and physical attraction to gain the upper hand. Nona's thirst for power was fueled by sex, and as the villagers regarded her as nothing more than a physical prize for their own sexual appetites, she was ultimately undone by the same kind of negative sexual energy she sought to wield against Captain Kirk.

By Any Other Name
Sexual Situation: Sexual Jealousy
StarDate: 4657.5

"A rose by any other name would smell as sweet"
– William Shakespeare

Imagine—You need to return home and the space journey employing a Federation starship will take 300 years to complete. After responding to a planetary distress call, the Enterprise is hijacked by the Kelvans—highly advanced aliens who are maintaining a humanoid appearance for logistical convenience. As the trip back to their home Empire progresses, the Kelvans find themselves becoming more and more human and need to restrain themselves from allowing the human equation to unbalance and overtake them.

The Kelvans, longing for home, need to travel vast intergalactic distances by utilizing a humanoid designed and engineered starship. Though outwardly appearing perfectly homosapien, they really aren't human beings. They neatly assume human appearance and the matching physical scale of Earth men and women to facilitate a successful hijacking of Captain Kirk's Enterprise. Spock, after engaging in a brief probing mind meld with Kelvan Kelinda, determines that these beings in actuality are much larger, and possess hundreds of tentacle-like limbs.

Squidbillies on the Enterprise?

Like some ragtag band of refugee storybook elves, fairies and gnomes—or even perhaps a few hell spawned demons—the Kelvans remind us of the *other*. The odd creature or entity—who must successfully absorb or experience the important customs of humanity to fully understand our complex species.

Like Ariel the mermaid in Disney's *The Little Mermaid*, or Darryl Hannah in *Splash* with Tom Hanks, the Kelvans in assuming human form have now accelerated their transformation into mortal creatures. And like both Ariel and Hannah's characters, human emotions tend to complicate things.

All the technology and wisdom in the universe may not be able to properly handle the tidal wave-like onslaught of emotions, if one isn't used to being drenched by such intense feelings; like the angry toddler who can't exercise impulse control when faced with a choice of toys, or the puberty encased teenager who now must deal with feelings of a crush or the ripping out of one's heart from rejection or jealous pangs from a competitor's advance on an object of love. Lust and romance are inextricably intertwined and often can be downright messy.

The dangerous love triangle which develops between Kirk, Kelinda and Rojan may be fabricated by the fact that the Kelvans appear much like wide eyed children dealing with raging emotional roller coasters for the first time, but it's more than authentic to the participants involved within the romantic tinged trio.

After finding Kelinda being schooled in the ways of romance through the fine art of deep french kissing Kirk, Rojan flips out in a rage of volcanic jealousy. How can this advanced alien race be acting so embarrassingly human? How can they be at the mercy of things a high school senior would stumble over, yet probably handle better? Like so much to be discovered when exploring in *Star Trek*, the aliens are the mirror Roddenberry and his writers would hold up to us each week. We can see through their flashy, weird or mundane, but all too familiar actions just how immature or self destructive we humans become when we allow our emotions to run rampant over our lives and loves.

In the end, the Kelvans realize they can't ever go home again. They are now much too infected by the human virus, and so they return to the planet where Kirk and crew found them. We can't help but wonder just what hybrid race will arise from the Kelvans going back to the planet they were marooned on; surely more human than Kelvan, but still far more Kelvan to live harmoniously among human beings on Earth?

For The World Is Hollow and I Have Touched The Sky
Sexual Situation: Alien & Human Romance & Marriage
StarDate: 5476.3

> *Shortly after Dr. McCoy reveals he's suffering from a terminal disease which gives him only about a year to live, a barrage of ancient missiles is detected heading towards Enterprise. Easily dispatching them, the Federation starship turns its attention on the place of their origin—a huge asteroid named Yonada—which is now on a deadly collision course with a Federation planet.*

If you knew you had only a year left to live, what would you do with your remaining 365 days of life?

Would you try to live the rest of your life to its fullest? If you were terminally ill, and a great romantic love came into your life, would you leave your family, friends and career to go off and live with them in a strange new place? For Dr. McCoy, these philosophical questions become much more than mental gymnastics or stimulating academic banter about how one deals with the terminal nature of living as a mortal man. Certain death is impending for all of us—it's just a matter of how and when.

Bones doesn't ever give his good friend J.T. Kirk a real run for his money in the lusty romance department, but considering who he falls in love with in this episode, it's clear the good Dr. McCoy is definitely no slouch as a sometime ladies' man. Natira, from the generational ship

Yonada, is a beautiful woman with an entire world—dysfunctional as it may be—to look after, but her focus becomes divided by McCoy's arrival.

Natira, as the leader of this massive super computer controlled generational craft, is a busy woman. She of course (as do all the others on Yonada) buys into the nifty notion that theirs is a blessed kingdom culture—a real planet or world, and not a product of high tech artifice. When someone does act independently and display that their brain is working on a higher level, they are punished—sometimes even fatally.

Yonada's high priestess also is gifted with the freedom which others below her station in their society are not. She can freely choose who her mate is; in this case, she has chosen the terminally ill Starship physician Leonard McCoy.

Natira has never been to Earth, but if she knew of the older, more traditional convention of male and female roles when it comes to courtship, she may be celebrating her power in this regard even more. The two become man and wife in a joining ceremony full of flourish and symbolism—McCoy is now a married man.

Natira, through her own cultural upbringing on Yonada, but perhaps more importantly, by the isolation and artificiality of a living environment on an asteroid sized generational spacecraft, has no doubt encouraged the necessity of unconventional customs. If this is a native cultural aspect of traditional Yonada society, we'll never know—but it doesn't matter. Here, considering McCoy's predicament, it becomes both romantic and plot convenient. After all, an alien dying man—fresh from a foreign world and his faraway Federation—picking out his own love and/or future bride may not go over too well with an alien culture, sociologically advanced or not.

Dr. McCoy's decision to toss his old life in favor of a new one because of such an intense sexual and romantic attraction to the lovely Natira proves to be the remedy he'd been looking for all along. It enables him to find the medical cure he needed, though in the end, it denies him of the simple life he may have been craving to live now for years.

Plato's Stepchildren
Sexual Situation: Sexual Sadism, Humiliation & Voyeurism
StarDate: 5784.2

Ancient Greece full of bitter, perverted psychokinetic abusers who tortured the 'lower classes' with acts of forced sexual humiliation?

Plato could never have intellectualized these merciless telekinetic sadists. However, when Kirk and crew embark on an urgent mission, they must deal with the superior minded aliens called Platonians. Soon, it's a heady battle of the minds—with one of the smallest and seemingly most vulnerable of beings becoming an example and even an ideal in admirable humanity to emulate for all involved.

Greek civilization—the ancient romantic era of Plato and Aristotle—is a time in Western history to be greatly admired and even emulated. The liberating social and cultural ideals of that golden landmark time are still influencing us and are still a great focus of scholarly study. The Platonic Ideal or Platonic Idealism still draws scores of students to pour over and scrutinize its intricacies. The Plato emulating students or Platonians whom Kirk and Enterprise crew encounter are far and away from such a mind expanding school which nurtures critical thinking and philosophy.

In short, these Platonians are more freaks than anything else.

Is Parman, the head Greek wannabe, who acts far more like a Roman emperor in his tyrannical attitude and violent, ruthless discipline, the ultimate bully? Or has the irresistible allure of such a sweeping power to make your thoughts manifest themselves into reality been too much for him to use and not be corrupted to a point of abuse? Like Gary Mitchell, Charlie Evans and Trelane—have Captain Kirk and his crew met yet another despotic godhead who is merely flexing his magical powers to impress and intimidate?

Unfortunately, Kirk, Spock and McCoy find that this time they are truly outnumbered. The alien Platonians are actually a group of several snobbish tin gods. This time they aren't dealing with merely one out of control powerhouse. All the aliens can perform telekinetic terror, so it's like a gang of gods run amok trying to outdo and outperform each other when it comes time to use their nifty mind moving parlor tricks. It's sort of like being in a room full of Stephen King *Carries*—each one fueled by a motivation to use their powers as entertainingly and as abusively as possible.

But above all the others stands Parman. As the Platonian leader, he's the most powerful mentalist of them all and the most merciless. When he takes on Kirk for barging into his chambers—showing off the full brunt of his irresistible mental influence—it's a withering display of mental directed physical abuse.

As a horrified Alexander watches, he forces the Captain of the Enterprise to repeatedly slap himself in the face. The dwarf Alexander looks on, pitying the only person who has shown him any level of respect or friendship now being reduced to a freak show attraction—being forced to beat himself almost senseless. The scene plays as powerfully disturbing, even more so than any full fledged knock out drag out fist fight Kirk has ever found himself in. This time, Kirk kicks his own ass.

And then later comes the now legendary **kiss**.

Jim Kirk's big kiss with Lt. Uhura is now legendary for so many reasons. It's one of those shared TV moments which becomes a collective cultural touchstone for both fans and also scholars of classic American television. Even those who never watched any or much *Dallas*, with Larry Hagman, knew about the international furor over the 'Who shot JR?' storyline. Moments like the finale of *The Sopranos* or Lucy Ricardo's giving birth to Little Ricky on *I Love Lucy* are similar milestones.

Here, actress Nichelle Nichols as Lt. Uhura was forced to kiss her superior officer, Captain Kirk, and though it may sound romantic or even pleasant, it's neither of those things.

That Kirk and Uhura are not sincerely moving to a voluntary romantic tempo in their embrace and kiss at first appears to slightly cheat or at least remove some of the human passion of the moment. Indeed, the two are now dressed up like ancient Greeks themselves and are clutching breathlessly at one another in front of an audience because they enjoy necking for the sake and pleasure of the aliens' sadistic voyeurism.

We feel sympathy over such a pairing being orchestrated by the sadistic Platonians. But if we listen carefully, the dialogue between the two more than implies they are making the best of the stressful situation. Uhura even talks about how often on the Enterprise during an emergency, she'd be 'scared to death', but would look over to her Captain and her fears would fade away. Is this an indication that Uhura and Kirk could have had a romantic chemistry after all?

What's often forgotten about the stirring scene is that Kirk and Uhura share the awkward romantic theater along with Spock and Nurse Chapel—both of them also acting under the telekinetic bonds. The Platonians force Chapel to be held tenderly by Spock, and she's so mortified—because of her deep feelings of love for Spock—since her intimate vulnerability for Spock is now being exposed so completely on such a public and humiliating level.

In some ways, the Spock and Chapel pairing may be even more sensational—a hybrid human alien embracing his fellow crew member, suffering from the bad romance yearnings of her unrequited love.

In truth, before the William Shatner and Nichelle Nichols forced liplock on *Trek*, an interracial kiss came before on American TV. Robert Conrad's character, James T. West (those James T.'s do get around don't they?) shared a kiss with Filipina-American actress Pilar Seurat, on an episode of *The Wild Wild West*. Shatner and Nichols, with their famed bout of tongue wrestling, would become the first white man and black woman to kiss on American broadcast television.

In Europe, in the United Kingdom, the BBC didn't air the episode for years—until 1994—because of 'sadistic elements'

Wink Of An Eye
Sexual Situations: Forced Enslavement for Breeding Stock
StarDate: 5710.5

What if a whole day's events transpired in the time it took to simply blink your eyes? The Enterprise is invaded by a race of alien beings from the planet Scalos who move so quickly, their entire day flashes by instantaneously—over chronologically in the span of one of our Earthly seconds. Captain Kirk's combat dilemma: How can you defeat an enemy who looks upon your speediest actions as if you're frozen still?

In the surreal world of comic books, Superman, or the Man of Steel, and the Flash are the fastest men alive. Make that the fastest *extraterrestrial* (Kryptonian) on Earth and the fastest human being on the planet respectively. Anyway, the fact is these fictional men can move faster than a hummingbird tanked up on a case of Red Bull. When the Enterprise is invaded by super speedy types like those DC superheroes, it's a wonder how Kirk and crew could ever contend with such irresistible warp speed-like power.

Some fans, and the more nitpicky or creatively challenged among the professional reviewers, have found the science, or more precisely, the science fiction here, lacking weight or patently unbelievable in this episode. I suppose those same killjoys cringe when the Flash speeds by on a rescue or simply can't watch when Superman does something lickety split.

Phasers move at the speed of light, so how could Deela (Kathie Browne) have moved aside so swiftly to safety when Kirk fires on her, they screech. Blah Blah Blah. Can I skip this boring lecture on stuffy reality, Professor Truthy?

As is so often the case with *Star Trek*, science, science fiction, drama and pop culture art meld together seamlessly. The suspension of disbelief may be much more required to convincingly buy the Scalosians' hyper accelerated lifestyle, but if you can't do that effectively, you also can't enjoy much of the most popular sci-fi and or comic book movie and TV fun. More than that, you miss the dramatic point of the episode entirely.

Despite Kirk's practical need to restore his ship and himself, Deela, Queen of Scalos leaves a definite impression on him. This may not be a storybook love story like Edith Keeler from *City On The Edge Of Forever*, or even someone as romance ready like old flame Dr. Carol Marcus, but it's clear Jim Kirk is more than merely fond of the Scalosian queen.

In fact, unlike more than a few episodes where Kirk merely flirts with a woman or tries to bed an exotic hottie but fails, here he scores majorly with Deela. In fact, when Rael comes in and attacks Kirk—after Deela and he have a rock and roll in the hay—in a jealousy fueled rage, we can see that the Scalosian nature in terms of romantic envy hasn't been dulled by their sped up state.

Although the Scalosians can't be seen as misunderstood, the desperation in saving their fading race makes them easy to pity. Turning the Enterprise into a humongous frozen sperm bank is certainly a high minded, if a singularly bizarre or even ludicrous concept, but hey, they need new genes to infuse their race, so why the hell not.

Why a few prime specimens like Kirk, Chekov or a few dozen red shirts wouldn't be enough to just kidnap for breeding nags as a lingering question. But then, of course, we wouldn't have the raging Rael needed for his tech expertise in setting up the deep freeze device, nor his violent confrontation with Captain Kirk.

Ultimately, as he bids her farewell in the transporter room, Kirk tells Deela there's not much he'd rather do than to stay with her, except staying alive. Though their love affair may have been as rushed as the hyper accelerated plot device, this was a good old fashioned love story. Large credit for the tale's effectiveness goes to the fantastic performance of actress Kathie Browne as the haughtily royal, yet still magnetic Deela. She makes yet another love affair for Kirk seem somehow fresh, unique and above all memorable.

To the naysayers, to the thoroughly unromantic, to the just plain coldly logical or boring who can't see the holographic forest through the replicated trees: Calm down and take a look at this tale again. It just may relax you enough to stop feeling so darned *hyper* about life and love in general.

The Empath
Sexual Situations: Empathic Physical Torture—BDSM
StarDate: 5121.5

> *Starship Enterprise travels to Minara II, a planet where Federation scientists have been conducting research, but when an away team beams planetside, they have trouble locating the men. As Captain Kirk, Spock and Dr. McCoy continue to search for the missing personnel, they're taken captive by an alien duo who conduct a series of torturous experiments on them. The motive? To determine if an entire race is worthy of being saved from destruction by gauging the emotional reactions and choices of a female empath named Gem—who's forced to watch the torture and heal the men with her wondrous empathic power.*

Empathy. It's an ability to relate to someone so accurately you are close to feeling what they are feeling—or at least more understanding of their emotional state. We all know people like that in our lives. Those around us who are more empathic than others when it comes to our emotional intelligence. In the *Star Trek* universe, Counselor Deanna Troi stationed on Captain Picard's Enterprise 1701-D, is half Betazoid and half Human. Her Betazoid DNA enables her to feel what others feel, and she'd offer valuable counsel to her commander and crewmates.

Before the Betazoid Counselor Troi, there was another empath, Gem.

Played by actress Katherine Hays (*As The World Turns*), Gem was as mysteriously silent as Troi was magnetically loquacious. The most important difference lay in the physical healing which Gem could facilitate on the injured, sick, or even those who were dying. While Deanna Troi listened to her patients and challenged the sincerity or veracity of alien diplomats or despotic rulers, Gem simply made right what went wrong for one who was in pain or suffering from an illness. Like some healing angel sent from a heavenly therapeutic realm, Gem employed her expressive body language and she'd mime her altruistic intentions so to convey to Kirk, Spock and Dr. McCoy her willingness to help and heal them.

For the caged Starfleet trio, Gem becomes both savior and sadist. The judge and judgmental aliens, the Vians, are the true architects of their torturous imprisonment. Mad scientists or impassioned intellectuals searching for the truth? Does it really matter with this level of torture going down?

Gem is merely a laboratory rat, an exploited pawn, but her presence makes the three know the continual pain they'll keep facing, followed by the near instantaneous healing provided by her empathic ability.

What may mostly set apart this seemingly non -sexual episode is just how the Vians 'experiment' on and set up Gem for the testing of her altruism and worthiness to be saved along with her scrutinized race. On its face, it's a fairly simple visual: It appears as if the Vians are employing good old fashioned bondage, domination and sadomasochism.

The S&M or BDSM community prides itself as being well versed in such a duality of pain and pleasure. Like the surreal literary sex of what's fictitiously explored in the popular novel *Fifty Shades of Grey*, participants in the sexual liberation and sexual satisfaction of engaging in causing a romantic partner pain, denial or combinations of these revel in raw emotional and physical extremes.

It's like a Yin Yang of pleasure and pain, where there's a little pain in your pleasure and vice versa. Captain Kirk, Dr. McCoy, Mr. Spock and Gem never engage in sexual entanglements per se, but the kinky Vians provide more than a buffet of classic BDSM style scenarios.

Bondage and S&M, after a fashion, makes a startling appearance here as the probing Vians physically abuse the trio to see if Gem will be selfless in her outreach to heal the physical damage. It is as if an alien kink duo has orchestrated this little S&M show for self indulgent reasons and is masquerading it as something more clinical. Could such a technologically advanced race have utilized other measures to inflict similar damage without putting on such a BDSM freak show? Sure, but then we wouldn't have such a titillating tale of flesh based torture to savor for those of us fascinated by such fare. Or maybe since the physical damage and abuse is so raw and natural, it helps to set up something deeply emotional and primal in Gem, thereby releasing the full force of her empathic nature and abilities.

In Europe, in the United Kingdom, the BBC didn't air the episode for years—until 1994—because of 'sadistic elements'

Elaan Of Troyius

Sexual Situations: Aphrodisiac, Arranged Marriage & Love Potion
StarDate: 4372.5

Can an arranged marriage bring peace to two worlds desperately in need of ending bloody warfare? When Kirk's Starship Enterprise must transport an alien royal to her politically motivated marriage to a stranger in order to the end hostilities between two races, he learns how much chaos a spoiled leader can bring forth to all around her. The pampered leader, called the Dohlman, not only stabs the envoy from the enemy planet, but the crocodile tears she cries act like a love potion to men—and she's crying up a storm in the vicinity of Captain James T. Kirk.

Helen of Troy. She late, great but forever eternal of the ancient Greek myth and lovely legend boasting such unparalleled Earthly human beauty, that her exquisite face was capable of *launching a thousand ships*. It's an unforgettable story, a real romantic yarn which nearly every school kid knows, and nearly every lover of Greek mythology savors and holds dear. Like the glorious giddiness of the tale, the Enterprise crew encounters Elaan, the Dohlman of Troyius, an alien royal who may be best described as capable of launching a thousand heated arguments.

James T. Kirk has tangled with many rough men, sparred with a bunch of bizarre beings and had to deal with a few truly tough women. Elaan, though not the most physically strong specimen around, makes up for it by throwing her weight around to the point of being completely abusive and even violent.

Indeed, when she is displeased with the Troyian ambassador, Petri, she tries to do away with him by stabbing the poor guy. Kirk realizes he must use all of his Starship commander powers and strategy, but more importantly his own Kirk charisma on her, and that's when things get decidedly entertaining for all interested parties.

Keeping in mind the cosmic complexities surrounding the important political elements which Starfleet has entrusted him with safeguarding, Kirk proceeds to 'tame' if you will the wildly tempestuous Elaan. In this way, she can at the very least be made to be more cooperative—or hopefully not kill or maim anyone else—before being dropped off at her pre-arranged wedding to a Troyian nobleman.

Elaan doesn't waste much time in trying to do the same nasty thing to Kirk that she did to Petri, and that's when the sci-fi tale morphs into something more like a fairytale.

We learn that Elasian women possess a secret romantic WMD at their disposal—a love potion-like substance which captures the throbbing heart of any man exposed to the stuff. What's so convenient about the libido boosting stuff is that it's plentiful and easy to administer to the romance target, since it's contained in an Elasian woman's tears.

After a physical melee with Kirk, while the Dohlman pretends to feel sorry for herself about how she alienates all those who may care for her, she begins to sob pathetically. Kirk caresses the Dohlman's face, and as he does so, he absorbs Elaan's tears through his skin. He's now under the romantic whammy of her biochemical love drug.

Like being shot with Cupid's arrow oozing in a liquid saline form, Kirk soon experiences more than merely a mild connection with Elaan. If the Dohlman had cried around Spock or say McCoy, the Vulcan's control of the former and the more romantically reserved or inexperienced nature of the latter may have meant a far different outcome.

As it stands, Kirk ends up throwing off the magic of the biochemical aphrodisiac by holding on to a love far greater than one woman. Kirk's most alluring romance is, has been and always will be something far greater than a biological love affair: **Starship Enterprise.**

For that overpowering obsession, there's no cure for the addicted Captain Kirk, only the continued adventurous lifestyle of seeing what's out there…

Whom Gods Destroy

Sexual Situations: Shape Shifter Sex, Sexual Violence Psychotic
StarDate: 5718.3

Thankfully, the criminally insane are now a vanishing breed in the United Federation of Planets, but they're not yet completely extinct. On planet Elba II, an asylum has been established to care for and cure the last of these dangerously ill criminals. After Enterprise brings a wonder drug which promises to cure the mental ravages of the tortured inmates, it's discovered that the facility's head physician has been incarcerated himself—convincingly replaced by a shape shifting, legendary former Starfleet captain, Garth of Izar.

Enter Garth of Izar. Garth may be a raving lunatic capable of any violent action which will serve his completely insane plans, but he's entertainingly theatrical. Beyond his dramatic flourishes, he has one of those catchy, stage savvy names that we can't help but remember. *Garth GaGa—Led Garth—Alien Ant Garth—Wayne & Garth*—party on, you wacky shape shifter!

Sadly, for Captain James T. Kirk, not only does he remember Garth of Izar's name as that of a legendary Starfleet captain to be looked up to, admired and even emulated, but for Kirk as a cadet, Garth was a real personal inspiration to him. Now, Garth is a far different man.

The real weird sexcapade of this episode comes in the green magic and the allure of the Orion Sex slave girl. Instead of experiencing the smoldering animal magnetism that is usually accompanied by such a kinky presence, this one would give anyone second thoughts about having a one night stand with such a thoroughly disturbed individual.

Played by lithe actress Yvonne Craig—best known as Commissioner Gordon's daughter and Batgirl from the Adam West camp fest, the 1960's *Batman*—Marta carries on her race's tradition of the Orion's no holds barred sexuality on parade, but since she suffers from a destabilizing mental illness, she's a dangerous one to bed indeed. Kirk, being the sexual explorer that he always is, finds this out directly.

You see, Marta makes Glenn Close's character in *Fatal Attraction* look normal side by side.

"He is my lover and I have to kill him!"

Marta cries her romantic proclamation in anguish—making sense only to her own warped logic of love—as she tries to kill Kirk and Spock stops her. But of course when you're dealing with a shape shifting villain, you never know who exactly is who. In this case, Spock turns out to be Garth posing as the Vulcan, and things go wacky yet again in playing ID check without any way of unmasking the real deal.

The episode's core story deals mostly in the complex, and still practiced even today in our modern, more educated and accepting social climate, stigmatization of the terribly and criminally mentally ill. Marta may appear to be an enticing sexual symbol, even irresistible, but her inability to distinguish reality from her poisonous delusions make her sexual advances just as deadly as a phaser or razor sharp blade.

Captain Kirk has faced many a dangerous foe while galaxy going and planet hopping. He's gone toe to toe with towering and glowering Klingons, faced combat trained warriors in alien arenas, but one of his fiercest foes had to be the desolate Marta, who fixated on him and felt she had to do away with him after making out with the dashing Starfleet captain—like some green skinned black widow spider.

The Mark of Gideon
Sexual Situations: Overpopulation, Birth Control
StarDate: 5423.4

> *Planet Gideon boasts an idyllic society, even an apparent paradise. The world's inhabitants live wonderful lives for many a year, but is this utopia really what it seems to be? When Enterprise makes a diplomat visit to Gideon for the leaders to engage in talks to recruit the planet into the Federation, Captain Kirk mysteriously disappears in a transporter malfunction. In truth, he's been captured and is being held in a mirror replica Starship Enterprise by the aliens to facilitate a deadly solution to their overpopulation problem.*

Here's a dramatic examination of a serious or even deadlier side of the human sexual equation, with sociological ramifications that impact an entire country, or even the whole world.

Although the most populous country on our own planet, The People's Republic of China, has slightly relaxed its one child only policy to keep its numbers in check, it's still woefully crowded. In such a physically large country as China, it may not be felt as keenly as, say, the population or crowding problems of Japan, or India, but the need for geographic expansion in such cases—or a decrease in population rate—must be exercised.

Birth control may be a sensitive issue for the religious minded or politically motivated among us, but the simple fact is that unprotected sexual activity leads to procreation and can lead to an out of control population growth. For the people of Gideon, it has gotten to the point of no return—they must stem the explosive population numbers. As the compelling sci-fi twist, the inhabitants of the planet Gideon exist in a kind of global clean lab—where no germs can infect them, thereby making illness and death nearly unknown.

Then there is the unlikely romance between Odona and Captain Kirk. It doesn't last long; just enough to get the damaging job done effectively.

Odona courts Kirk as if they're young lovers on a carefree quest for romance, not the shocking secret act she's hiding from him: Becoming infected with a virulent disease to help curb Gideon's population. When Kirk and Odona kiss passionately while on the fake Enterprise's bridge, it's highly symbolic of the whole core story of the dark tale. The problem for Gideon is that far too many people engaged in far too much procreation because they were promised the miracle of near immortality through the advancement of their miraculous science.

Young Odona takes full advantage of this wonderful freedom. She's finally free—in all possible ways. She can move about freely on a spacious ship and she isn't fearful of bumping into yet another of her race.

She's free to romance a handsome man like Kirk and she's free to try to contract a virus that will then help free her entire world from the oppression of their suffocating overpopulation. We may know that there's more to this free for all than meets the eye, but we can't help but get lost in the spontaneous glee the joyous Odona is feeling.

Though the episode maintains an always serious, even sober look at the damage of population growth run rampant, the setup of the famed Lothario Captain Kirk may be more obvious or glaring here. While it's true Odona may have contracted the virus by just being close to Kirk—that's certainly plausible in our own 21st century medical knowledge of disease transmission—the kiss seals the deal and also seals the assumptions of the Gideons. How could they know Kirk would definitely kiss Odona—thereby accelerating the passing of the virus? Starship Enterprise boasts a reputation around the galaxy, and apparently, James T. Kirk boasts an even bigger cosmic street cred as love leader for his many galactic, romantic conquests.

The Gamesters of Triskelion

Sexual Situations: Slaves Bred for Games, Rape, Humanoid Breeding Stock, Love
StarDate: 3211.7

Planet Triskelion. As Enterprise orbits the planet of Gamma II, to complete a standard inspection tour of an unmanned station, Kirk, Lt. Uhura and Ensign Chekov try to beam down for the mission, but are instantly yanked off the transporter pads by an unknown force. The away team soon find they're the newest recruits in a no holds barred fighting game. These Starfleet officers will now live out their remaining days as 'game thralls'—or combat trained slaves to fight in a spectator bloodsport arena.

Let the games begin! *Sex games?* Well, no, not quite. But love and sex does enter into the pugilistic equation.

The gargantuan sporting success of MMA or *Mixed Martial Arts* and the Ultimate Fighting Championship are our modern culture's answer to the gladiator fighting forms found in arenas from Earth's ancient times. In Rome particularly, the gladiator lifestyle flourished and is associated with the legendary Roman Coliseum. Such gladiatorial similar sport can be found in the ancient peoples of the Maya, Aztec, Asia—and in many other civilizations. Humans have been pitted against each other as pugilistic combatants in fighting contests since the earliest times.

Even the highly abuse charged and bloody carnival gone amok atmosphere of pitbull dog fights or cock fighting harkens back to the notion of one being pitted against another—mano a mano—the strong, clever and most ruthless shall survive the primal struggle.

MTV, the pop culture media powerhouse, even created a claymation or stop motion styled television show called *Celebrity Death Match,* which while played strictly for laughs, hit home on the notion of how compelling it is for humans to watch other humans beat each other senseless. This, while perhaps not always consciously nor directly observable, undoubtedly ties into notions of sexual domination and submission.

In the thrall universe, Kirk is even granted a wildly sexually charged and alluring thrall trainer. Shauna, played by the generously endowed actress Angelique Pettyjohn, exemplifies every notion of a fantasy maiden who is as quick with the fighting weapon as she is with her impressive biological attributes. Pettyjohn may not be subtle in the way she approaches her character's dominant sexuality, but the broad nature of the arena in which she encounters Kirk demands such overlording, titillating theatricality.

One interesting note is that—in art imitating life—Angelique Pettyjohn is also an adult film actress. So considering that, the fictional pornography of the Shauna character isn't exactly far afield from the tone and timbre of her other career pursuits.

Perhaps more than any other 'Kirk chases alien hottie woman love tale' episode, this one surprisingly feels more romantic or even more authentic. Shauna is near childlike in her ignorance of the exploration of human love, and so when Kirk becomes her teacher, the lack of sophistication in her or any sexual artifice is both refreshing and inspiring.

True romance or just clever tactic on Kirk's part to escape alive? Watch the episode again and decide. This much is well beyond debate. Kirk explains 'love' to the beautiful thrall Shauna, and although he has to betray her by tricking her into caring for him and being physical with him, it's clear Kirk has some real feelings for the alien beauty.

Like a romantic themed martial arts film, ala *Bloodsport, Return of the Dragon, Crouching Tiger, Hidden Dragon* or *Enter The Dragon*, where charismatic fighters Bruce Lee, Chuck Norris, Jet Li or Jean Claude Van Damme must confront a beautiful lover in the brutal combat arena, Shauna must face Kirk in the final battle—a battle for his very life and for his starship crew's freedom.

Kirk has gambled with the thrall owning Gamesters, and if he wins, he wins it all for his crew and Shauna's thralls. If he loses, he'll help to make his entire crew into thralls. Shauna has been hurt by Kirk—she feels that all he told her was a lie. Her feelings of betrayal get the better of her, and Kirk's finely honed warrior instinct wins the day—sparing blood and avoiding a deathmatch.

As the ever masculine, eternally studly Captain from Earth beams away, Shauna says goodbye to him and says that she will remember, as tears flow down her face. She looks up into the camera, which ends with a magnificent bird's eye view crane shot climbing high into the sky. It's a fitting and most memorable end to this all too brief love affair.

Requiem for Methuselah

Sexual Situation: End of Innocence, Artificial Intelligence Sexual Imprinting
StarDate: 5843.7

After the crew of the Enterprise are stricken with a deadly disease, Rigelian Fever, the Federation Starship must search for the only known way to concoct the cure—a rare mineral called Ryetalyn. However, when a planet is found containing the needed substance, the crew encounter two humans far from home; Flint, a mysterious human and his equally enigmatic adopted daughter, Rayna, who seem resistant to reveal their true identities. Before long it's suspected that Flint's mystery may be far more complex and fantastic than anyone could ever dream of and that most shocking of all, he may have been alive now for thousands of years.

Immortality. But at what price? For our man Flint—aka *Da Vinci, Alexander, Merlin, Lazarus*—et al—all of his vast knowledge, calming wisdom and assured mastery over advanced technology and even life and death is all but naught when it comes to understanding mortal love and human companionship. Simply put—the man who never dies needs to romance a mate who is as culturally sophisticated and as long lived as he.

Yet again, Captain Virility takes over the limelight on center stage. We have another episode which centers on Kirk's sizeable libido. It's wonderfully romantic to subscribe to his old fashioned notions of love at first sight, but the simple fact is that the exotic Rayna greatly arouses him physically. His powerful sexual urge for her may indeed lead to a more substantive or mature affection or even real love down the line, but for now, Captain Kirk's legendary lover loins are set on full power, and Rayna's shields aren't exactly raised.

But that physical moment, no matter how fiery and erotic, fades for everyone. Those animal urges can't last or burn brightly forever, and so Kirk—perhaps in some ways as lonely and detached as a Flint, a man who will never know death—succumbs to the far more powerful motivation of them all—*love*. Ultimately, Kirk's immediate and all too familiar lasciviousness gives way to affection and then to a passionate love—however short lived or cosmetic it may appear to be. Kirk may be in love with the notion of a young beauty so intelligent and so academically capable, yet as innocent as a pubescent teen when it comes to the romancing of men.

When Rayna, torn by the powerful love she feels for two powerful men, self destructs—a conflict so deep within her that it completely deprives her of her artificial life—we are taken away by the real poignancy of the fatal outcome. Her new found sense of love is so overwhelming to her fragile artificial psyche that it won't allow her to choose between the two feuding men. For *TNG* fans, it may remind them of the fragility of Data's android daughter, Lal (Hallie Todd), from the episode *The Offspring*, who also tragically expires at the end, pummeled fatally over her whirlpool of conflicting emotions.

Actress Louise Sorel—best known to daytime drama viewers for her role on NBC soap *Days of Our Lives*—plays the artificial genius Rayna as a worldly sophisticate in search of the one thing her books and computer databases can't properly teach or simulate for her—how to deal with the intellectually incomprehensible concept of *love*. Flint programmed her with curiosity and sensitivity, but could not reduce the intricate variables of the whimsy of love to an equation based formula.

An examination of this tale can't be rightfully done without invoking what had to be a huge influence on plot and characters for episode writer Jerome Bixby. *Forbidden Planet*, also a known influence for Gene Roddenberry in creating *Star Trek* in the first place, fairly bristles here at every turn. In comparing them, it's quite startling to see the plot parallels—aged scientist/genius is shepherding a young, beautiful girl, yet isolating her from the perils of the predation of the human male, while a robot of immense power guards over them on a desolate planet far from their Earthly origins.

Even the ending has a main character withering away from emotional angst. In the movie, Walter Pidgeon as commanding Morbius dies from an 'inner emotional conflict'—he can't reconcile destroying his daughter with the monster from his ID, while here, Rayna Kopek expires from her inner emotional turmoil; she can't reconcile choosing one love over another—thereby hurting or 'destroying' the one she doesn't pick.

Much has been made of the tale's finale scene—that of Spock healing his Captain of the wrenching hole Rayna's made in his heart. Kirk, seated at the desk in his quarters, exhausted from his romantic loss, hangs his head onto his hands. Spock watches over his Captain—who's finally fast asleep, yet we know he's still tortured in his dreams. McCoy enters and natters on about Flint being human now. *Who really cares, Bones? Is this really the time for such obvious and superior sounding exposition?*

But before he exits, southern genteel gentleman Doc Bones—always one to quickly put Spock into his logical loving place—reads him the riot act of how pathetic his Vulcan existence must be without the gory glory and the misery of love—since it's 'not written into his book.' McCoy, full of his sadistic and sarcastic self, exits and Spock promptly moves to his friend and mind melds with him. "Forget," intones the First Officer of The Enterprise.

On the surface, Spock's amnesia directive is self explanatory, even simplistic, yet what if Spock was serving up a dual capacity of Vulcan magic with his meld? Instead of merely infusing Kirk with soothing neurological fog, maybe he was also—heeding McCoy's critical words—reliving Kirk's romance with Rayna to bolster his own experiences. Perhaps Spock, by removing Kirk's grief and absorbing the memories into himself to hold, has healed his friend and brought himself one step closer to healing himself—the hybrid Vulcan Human who's always struggling to come to an appeasement or consolidation of the two facets of his personality.

The Way To Eden

Sexual Situation: Free Love—Hippie Love—Pursuit of Eden/Paradise
StarDate: 5832.3

Can hippies really change the world—or at least put us in such a state of cool and in the moment relaxation that nobody really cares if the world is what it is? That's the burning philosophical question a band of flower children pose to Captain Kirk and his hippie resistant crew. But these flower kids don't stop at just the intellectual or sociological pursuit of an idealized utopia. They hijack Starship Enterprise to actually go and find the embodiment of the mythical concept of paradise. Free love on a stolen starship? These hippies seem to want everything for free—since they simply and freely take what they feel is their cosmic destiny.

"Gonna crack my knuckles and jump for joy, I got a clean bill of health from Dr. McCoy!"

The campy music, though some would simply call it cringe inducing, alone in this one puts it in a class by itself—unfortunately, that's where many fans want to keep it—*all alone and unwatched in a dark and abandoned classroom somewhere.* Still, the free love aspect alone is certainly worth a trek to peruse our *Star Trek Sex.*

Taken as a purely camp exploration of the 1960's hippie movement—or at least *Star Trek's* filtered Hollywood TV take on it—the romp is simply just that—a heady head full of back to nature nonsense and new age philosophy, way before it was New Age. Shirley Maclaine or Deepak Chopra could have learned more than a merry metaphysical thing or two from these guys and gals.

Therapists Dr. Phil or Dr. Ruth may also have been at home alongside Doc Sevrin. Played by actor Skip Homeier, Sevrin comes across as a larger than life mish mash of Charles Manson and Timothy Leary. He's a man of science—in fact he is a genius in communications and sound theory—but his intense charismatic influence so enraptures his band of followers that it seems to blind them to anything but mindless obedience to his cause—the pursuit of Eden.

Is the pursuit of paradise—an Eden where all dreams or desires come true—simply an exercise or excuse to be the purveyors of free love? These days the ramifications of having multiple partners—not to mention high pregnancy rates of single moms—is well known statistically and tracked for decades since this episode aired back in 1969. Can a notion of free love—with all of its physical, financial and emotional weight—ever really be a practical reality in a society mature and advanced enough to want its citizens to practice their sexuality safely and responsibly?

Before the wide spread of fatal venereal diseases like AIDS—although syphilis and herpes and the like had no doubt been around in some form since humans started having sex—the free loving hippie movement exulted in the banter and beauty of bedding as many partners as possible. Indeed, even Kirk himself could be called the first practicing hippie Starship Captain in Starfleet—if only for his free love mentality and practice. But instead of embracing the free love of these hippies, Kirk wants them to conform and become a Herbert. What a hypocrite!

And then we have **Chekov**. Our resident Enterprise Russian wunderkind.

Walter Koenig never played the youthful Russian Ensign as a lover, player nor old fashioned kind of ladies' man—he had no reason to do so, since Pavel Chekov never really got the girl—but here he is now, and he can crow about being the object of a beautiful woman's affections.

It's an old flame that never really went out completely, and Irina Galliulin targets Chekov because she knows that his feelings are easily manipulated so she can obey her mentor, Sevrin, and help pilot the starship to the Eden her group yearns to find. Although much of the rekindling of the romance may be pretense on Irina's part, it's nice to see Chekov get the girl and be strong in his beliefs—even though he may come across more like a stuffed shirt Herbert than even his commanding officer.

Maybe Chekov could offer love lessons to Kirk?

All Our Yesterdays
Sexual Situation: Sexual Regression To Primitive Humanoid State
StarDate: 5943.7

Time travel made as easy as visiting a library and selecting a favorite 'book'? On planet Sarpeidon, after it is wholly doomed by an imminent supernova, its residents time warp and take refuge in various eras of the planet's history. When Spock, Kirk and McCoy are mistaken by the automated librarian as Sarpeidon natives, they are thrown into time warp portals, with Kirk alone in a witch hunting timeframe, and Spock and McCoy fighting for survival in the world's ice age.

The frigid North American Polar Vortex of 2014 may have not been a true ice age for much of the residents of the United States of America, but for many, it was like visiting the arctic and experiencing a deep freeze first hand. Many Americans would have loved to escape into a time portal to a warmer clime and time, but Mr. Atoz wasn't handy. So Spock and Dr. Mc-Coy ditched their Starfleet regulation Bermuda shorts, tossed their mai tais and decided to shack up with a woman named Zarabeth—played by Mariette Hartley.

It's a tale fraught with enough suspense and thrills to satisfy even a rabid action fan, yet Spock and Bones never venture out of Zarabeth's cave—so where's the meat? As in the best and most engaging Treks, this one is all about character development, and since T'Pring and Nurse Chapel aren't handy, Spock's Vulcan nature—devolved by Sarpeidon's primitive ice age environs—slowly morphs him from the cool, calm and collected human Vulcan hybrid, into a meat eating party animal.

Party on, caveman Mr. Spock! Party on, Captain Wayne! Unfortunately, for Captain Kirk, his historical era, while not frigid cold, merely has him fighting those who accuse him of witchcraft. Aside from a flirtation with a streetwalker type who helps get him incarcerated for witchery, there isn't much going on of note—certainly nothing sexually interesting.

"I'm behaving disgracefully. I've tasted animal flesh and I've enjoyed it. What is wrong with me?!"

Spock tells Zarabeth after she explains their food situation on the desolate, arctic world. Thus begins the realization for Spock and us that the supremely logical science officer is beginning to act far more like his ancient proto Vulcan or Neanderthal human ancestors.

Spock's in a cave and he's acting like a caveman.

Spock is devolving into a primal man—a more ravenous and robust humanoid in every way. His hunger isn't confined to simply eating the flesh of the animals of Sarpeidon for nourishment, since the usually vegetarian Vulcan has no access to native flora for food. His other hunger lies deep down and it's directed at Zarabeth.

We've seen Spock in the Vulcan version of 'heat' or time of mating. But in *Amok Time*, Spock came across more as a violent contestant fighting over winning the hand of the logical duplicity of the calculating T'Pring over choosing his commanding officer, Kirk. Now the only competitor for

Zarabeth's affections is Dr. McCoy and Spock fully knows how easily he can handle the older and far physically weaker ship's physician.

When Zarabeth says to Spock, "The Atavachron is far away. I think you come from some place farther than that," we know how true that is for the now rapidly devolving Vulcan in all possible ways. Not only has Spock travelled far in both time and space, but his mental state—his mind and Katra or Vulcan notion of the soul—has also become a traveller that's now experiencing physical desires and urges which are completely overwhelming to him.

Actress Mariette Hartley had something of a cottage industry in her TV guest roles as the girl who always got away, fresh from a passionate, impromptu love affair, or died—or in this case, was left in the frigid ice age of an ancient time. Her guest starring roles include *The Incredible Hulk* (for which she won an Emmy award)—opposite Bill Bixby—and, perhaps most famously to TV watchers, a series of Polaroid ads with actor James Garner of *The Rockford Files*. Hartley also guest starred in an episode of Garner's hit Rockford show. She's always the noble bridesmaid, but never the blushing bride.

What's perhaps most poignant and even heart wrenching is how much Spock, tied to his duty and his own timeline, loses when he says a final goodbye to Zarabeth. A brilliant and highly trained Starfleet officer would no doubt be wasted in such a useless time and place, but Spock could have been genuinely happy. Duty calls and Spock always dutifully answers.

Instead, he must go back to his Enterprise obligations, and to a familial duty and service bondage to his reputation as a famous diplomat's son. As Sarek of Vulcan's offspring, and the only Vulcan in Starfleet, he can't trivialize or do whatever he pleases with his life goals. For Kirk, there always seems to be another beauty conquest on yet another world, space vessel or space station, but for his buddy Spock, the chances at true romantic happiness is slim to none. Here it's denied him in spectacular style.

Turnabout Intruder

Sexual Situation: Gender Reassignment, Transgender Sexuality
StarDate: 5928.5

Responding to a distress call on planet Camus II, the Enterprise discovers several survivors of a severe medical emergency—radiation sickness. One of them is Dr. Janice Lester, a former girlfriend of Captain Kirk, whose relationship with the respected Starfleet commander soured because of debilitating jealousy. Lester desperately wanted and felt she more than deserved a Starship command. Now, with the assistance of alien tech, she'll get one, not by earning it, but by actually becoming Captain James T. Kirk.

Aired on June 3, 1969, this was the last first run episode of *Star Trek* to be aired on NBC.

Bruce Jenner, once heralded as one of America's greatest Olympic athletes, and then later as the Kardashians' step dad in the reality show which never seems to end, now seems poised to become the most famous symbol of the transgender community. Now known as Caitlyn Jenner, she appears as a courageous pioneer—as Chaz (Chastity Bono) before him— to try to educate the public about sexuality and the scale and the broad range gender continuum. As more people express who they really are in new and complex gender terms, our human species begins to understand the complexity of the whole notion of being a male or female who knows they are the wrong gender.

In the pioneering sci-fi arena and space opera universe created by Gene Roddenberry, things always get slightly more fun and fantastical.

Imagine pissing your ex off so much, they hatch a revenge plan so bizarre, so out of this world, it could only happen if they had access to super advanced alien technology found in an archaeological dig on a faraway planet. It's way weird, but simple to understand: your ex wants to target you for body swapping. Yes, the old soul switcheroo—the spirit shell game—the brain borrow. They want you back, yes, but for a wholly different and insidious reason.

Dr. Janice Lester definitely has a vendetta against her old flame, Captain Kirk. So deep and overpowering is this hunger for vengeance that she doesn't want to ruin his reputation, maim, kill him or hurt his loved ones—she wants to steal his entire life and reality by hijacking his body. Talk about payback!

Janice Lester wasn't always so vengeful, or even, arguably, psychotic. From the episode, it's more than implied she had always led an admirable life driven by the pursuit of obtaining higher education, exercising personal discipline and having purpose. She studied at Starfleet Academy and earned her doctorate, yet now she not only violates a plethora of Federation laws, she mars the essence and the spirit of camaraderie and humanism which Starfleet is known for encouraging in its members. Lester does all of this because in her mind, the powers that be at Starfleet are sexist or discriminatory against women achieving high level commands like that of a Starship commander.

Considering the era in which the tale was penned by writers Gene Roddenberry (Story) and Arthur H. Singer (Teleplay), it's no wonder the two scribes were highlighting the struggle with sexism by capable women who pursued their careers. The method used by the Hollywood artists of the day to spotlight such discrimination was social criticism by way of sci-fi and fantasy shows? You betcha.

But there are those who charge that because the Janice Lester character is written as mentally unstable, it sends a clear—or at least subtext message—that a woman wanting a more traditionally male role or job must be suffering from insanity.

As Spock would say, this is highly illogical.

What seems more the case is that Roddenberry (intentionally or not) was trying at the very least to paint a picture that the stresses of a confining society which buries such talented women with obscurity or mediocrity and deprives them of fulfilling their professional potential may just cause women such stress that they become mentally unstable. Why is this such an outrageously sexist notion? After all, both males and females even in our modern and less sexist culture of today, find high levels of stress in demanding careers. Couple this with a bad romance or break-up with a significant other, and it's not unusual nor blatantly sexist to argue that it could drive a woman, or man for that matter, over the edge.

Also there's a possibility that Janice Lester could be the queen of denial and rationalizing. Perhaps just as the academically challenged student—or the one who never studied adequately—calls the test too difficult or unfair, Lester is simply blaming the system for a sexist turn of events, when in reality it's her own shortcomings, blunders or lack of skill that explain her stalled career. Above all, anyone who's familiar with how much Gene Roddenberry fought for more prominent places for female cast members (his original first officer or Number One—Majel Barrett— was cast as a female) could never fairly make a charge that he was being sexist in his storytelling—at least consciously.

Let's more closely examine William Shatner's legendary—or for some, his infamous—performance in which he convinces us a woman's mind is inhabiting his male body.

Is his performance over the top? A little. Does he needlessly telegraph or too broadly portray predictable feminine ticks or even stereotypical characteristics? Perhaps. Does William Shatner give us an offensive acting turn screaming of intentional mockery? I really don't think so. The campy angle is also kind of weak and lacking in accuracy. Shatner is acting as if an emotionally disturbed woman has hijacked his body—to charge that he should have acted this in a subtle or more cool and collected way seems pretty naive.

The whole episode hinges upon body switching. Dozens of TV shows, movies—i.e. *Freaky Friday* with Jodi Foster—and even cartoons have played with this time worn plot device. Once the mind is switched into the new body, the actor or actress had better make sure we know there's something 'different' about this character, or we'll be confused—or worse still, fall fast asleep.

Today, we have far more sensitivity and public based education about the LGBT community and its great diversity. The lesbian, gay and bisexual community also counts individuals who are transgender or transsexual—those who are either actively pursuing gender reassignment or a sex change, and those who completely identify in their sexuality with those of the opposite sex. Even with all of our more modern health education, people are still confused or even completely ignorant about these sexual complexities.

Imagine what it was like during the 1960's for those who had to keep that kind of secret about themselves. While it's true the 60's were all about change, even radical transformation, the average American still didn't discuss the details of a sex change. Again, we can utilize and celebrate the miraculous lens of science fiction to ponder what kinds of transgender possibilities and progress could be enabled through technology which can bestow that kind of supremely complete physical transformation.

You could even make a case that a society that employed such a device could grant two individuals their desires by swapping two of different genders. No surgery necessary—just initiate a full, total mind swap and now both people have changed genders completely.

William Shatner's Starfleet Captain James T. Kirk shared the first interracial kiss with Nichelle Nichols as Lt. Uhura in the landmark episode, *Plato's Stepchildren*—yet in many ways, Bill Shatner was more of a real social pioneer in portraying a kind of transgender or transexual character in *Turnabout Intruder*.

Star Trek: The Motion Picture
Sexual Situation: Public Sexual Expression & Interaction, Oath of Celibacy

After a decade of syndicated TV success, unwavering fan adoration, popular science fiction fan conventions around the world and an aborted sequel series to be the flagship of a Paramount Pictures television network, Gene Roddenberry's starship of the imagination warped onto the silver screen in 1979. The crew were older, wiser and now joined by a mysterious alien named Ilia— a member of the Deltan race. Along with Commander William Decker, Kirk, Spock, McCoy, Scotty, Uhura, Sulu and Chekov raced against time to stop the ravaging V'Ger from absorbing everything which humanity holds dear into its ever growing and gargantuan informational matrix.

He's dead, Jim.

Can *Star Trek* ever really die? It's a legitimate question posed about the mortality of any franchise, no matter how apparently healthy and lucrative, but it's one which most fans today would probably scoff at believing. With five spin-off TV shows—I am counting the animated series—12 feature films, and hundreds of novels and comic books, fans are simply spoiled by such complete pop culture saturation. Gene Roddenberry's entertainment legacy seems assured of unassailable immortality. But it wasn't always so.

When the Robert Wise (*West Side Story* & *The Day The Earth Stood Still*) directed *ST:TMP* phaser blasted its way into theaters, the viewing public hadn't seen new live action *Trek* since 1969. Before then it was on the small screen in their living rooms. What would diehard fans think about this big budget adventure beamed up on the silver screen? How would critics receive the *Trek* mythology? Would new fans be lured into the theaters and welcomed into the IDIC fold, or would older ones be alienated or even reject it on the big screen?

What was clear about this big multiplex adventure from the get go was the new characters at the fore—Commander William Decker and Lt. Ilia. Portrayed by actor Stephen Collins and Persis Khambatta, the two were former flames reunited by duty and the overwhelming mission to contact and deal with V'Ger—a massively complex and enormous entity bent on either meeting its creator or exterminating all organic life in favor of a cyber matrix populated by digital simulations of people, things and other lifeforms.

Ilia isn't simply a beautiful woman—she's an alien lifeform, and one who was newly introduced to curious fans yearning to discover new life and new civilizations. She's of the Deltan race, and her people don't merely have sex with each other; they are highly sexual and promiscuous. Their entire society revolves around and utilizes sexual expression in virtually all matters of interaction.

Deltans are endowed with far more acute physical senses than human beings possess, and so it stands to reason their sexual instincts and practices are also more sophisticated. It's even been speculated that sex between a Deltan and a non-Deltan could result in insanity for the less sexually mature humanoid. Maybe Madonna, Lady GaGa or Miley Cyrus could stand up to having a roll in the hay with a Deltan, but us mere mortals would wither away in terror.

If this is the case, what do we make of the pairing of Decker and Ilia? Did the former lovers practice really careful safe sex in all aspects of their lovemaking? Or was the relationship restricted to a kind of careful, qualified celibacy—limiting the kinds of physical acts they performed on each other or even doing away with the physical element altogether? Since Deltans were the inspiration for the Betazoid race in *Star Trek: The Next Generation*, they had similar psychic abilities and talents. Deltans are empathic beings and can not only intuit the emotional states of other beings, but can also help to absorb or heal physical or emotional damage another is suffering from. Indeed, Ilia heals Chekov during the run in with V'ger, when he suffers a bad injury.

More than any other titillating detail about how the sex charged Deltans must carry themselves around sexually immature humans is the fact that they must swear an oath of celibacy while being stationed on a Starfleet vessel like Enterprise. Ilia announces this to Captain Kirk and assures Mr. Sulu that she's as safe as a human female because of this promise not to engage in sex with her backward human crewmates.

Did Decker—while he was stationed on Delta IV—learn a kind of biological sleight of hand to shield his body and mind from the powerful influences that Deltans can exert on others? If so, Decker could have built a little cottage industry for himself by advising others how to play nice and carefully around a Deltan—to maximize the potential pleasure and lessen any nasty side effects from a sexual union with them.

Whatever the case, whatever the ultimate standard and humanoid sexuality the two shared, when V'ger absorbs the two—Ilia already digitized into an artificial lifeform—it's surmised V'ger will learn much from the absolute power of their intense physical and romantic attraction for each other and the formidable love they share.

Star Trek VI: The Undiscovered Country
Sexual Situation: Trans Species Sex

"They have been our guides… our protectors… and our friends…."
ST:VI trailer narrated by Christopher Plummer

Finally, the original crew of fabled Starship Enterprise under James T. Kirk sail into their last adventure as a fully integrated crew. William Shatner's Kirk and James Doohan's Scotty, along with Walter Koenig as Pavel Chekov, would appear in the rousing opening of *Star Trek: Generations*, but Spock, McCoy and Uhura would never all join in together as a cohesive crew ever again.

For their last combined adventure, the galactic famous crew pit themselves against a renegade Klingon warrior of the old guard, played by a gloriously scenery chewing Christopher Plummer. Most entertaining of all, Captain Kirk will be served up the ultimate sexual Kobayashi Maru, after he's sentenced to prison for assassination. There, he finds old fashioned jailhouse romance—in the ever changing and morphing form of a shape shifting super model.

Even the most innocent kiss can pack a wallop of unintended consequences. James Kirk learns this bit of homespun wisdom after meeting a fellow inmate during his short, but memorable incarceration on the prison planet of Rura Penthe. Here, Kirk can't hack away or reprogram what amounts to a sexual Kobayashi Maru.

"I can't believe I kissed you!"
"Must have been your lifelong ambition."
– Kirk to Martia in Kirk form.

Beginnings and endings can be fraught with heavy emotional baggage. Remember going off to freshman college in your first year? How about reporting to boot camp in the military? Was mom wailing away in tears when she and dad said goodbye when dropping you off at summer camp? Similar emotional scenes revisit us when we come home from school, end our military service tour of duty or finish up a long term visit or relocation. Those sweeping milestones can charge us up with all kinds of emotion.

The *first* and the *last* in one's life—they task us.

It's interesting to note that with *Trek*'s first major motion picture entry, a main character experiences an emotionally charged romantic crisis. In *Trek*'s first big screen film, *ST:TMP*, it's Commander Decker encountering his old flame in Lt. Ilia. When they find themselves starting to reignite mutually smoldering feelings—courtesy of V'ger's less than subtle interference—a one time unified couple, then broken up by circumstance, renew a romantic relationship by being absorbed into the awe inspiring artificial consciousness of V'ger's vast digital existence.

In *Trek*'s big cinematic finale—the last all inclusive original crew outing—it's Mr. Spock firmly ensconced in the romance hot seat spotlight. Valeris, played by *Sex In The City*'s Kim Cattrall, is now Spock's current squeeze. It's not explained why Lt. Saavik—played by Kirstie Alley and Robin Curtis respectively in three previous films—isn't on the good Vulcan's arm anymore. Granted, theirs may have just been that of a mentor and student relationship, though after Saavik bonds with the horny teenage Vulcan in *ST:III*, things do get more physical. In any case—out with Saavik and in with Valeris.

We see a fully confident, in control and mature Spock handling a serious romantic relationship. This is not the young, even innocent Vulcan science officer we met during the Enterprise's five year mission—still wavering between the firmly drawn lines of his disparate cultures. This isn't a Spock trying to spoil the romantic trap set by the clever and conniving T'Pring. The half human, half Vulcan feels his affection and loyalty is being reciprocated in Valeris, and when it's revealed he's being played for a fool by a traitor he's romancing, we can feel and even see the finely controlled rage he's suppressing—albeit barely. Leonard Nimoy, in a rare display of acting out Spock's emotion, nearly physically assaults Valeris as he swats the phaser from her hand—the gun she'd intended to use as a weapon in her murder attempt.

Spock unfurls his rage for all to see. This now unhidden anger lies right at the heart of his relationship with Valeris. If he didn't care for her as much as he clearly does, he'd not be so willing to engage in such an uncharacteristic and public emotional outburst.

For Valeris, her pretense at something more substantial, intimate, real and lasting with the senior Starfleet luminary could be summed up with: *You always hurt the one you love.* Of course, when Spock engages in the mind meld—he's the one now who's truly in control. As he deeply probes his once beloved's mind, he doesn't employ the careful, precise control and gentleness he usually exhibits when engaged in this most personal of psychic interactions. Valeris moans in pain, eventually even screeches in anguish.

To the uncertain viewer, his visceral mind meld may appear as if Spock is initiating a violent mating ritual, or even mind raping Valeris. But this is no outlandish foreplay, nor a Vulcan's idea of S&M. Spock isn't evoking *Fifty Shades Of Grey* here. It's as painful for us to watch this interrogation spectacle as it is humiliating for her to have to experience.

Mind Melds are one thing—what of whole body melds (or at least liplocks) with a creature who's far different than 'she' appears to be?

Enter Martia.

During the 1990's, supermodel Iman still reigned at the height of her international fame and superstardom. She was one of an elite group of top models who set the standard for the fashion world's media crafted image of beauty for the famous, wealthy and globetrotting jet set. Although the producers first envisioned casting space opera familiar Sigourney Weaver of *Alien* fame as the character, it's now hard to imagine anyone else in the memorable role. With her exotic looks and voice, Iman hypnotizes as one of *Trek*'s most alluring beauties.

When Bones and Captain Kirk are processed at Rura Penthe—a brutal prison planet controlled by the now fading Klingon empire—it seems straightforward enough: Bleak, wretched and hopeless all apply to the lock-up. It's like Hollywood mashed up Guantanamo Bay and Alcatraz with Riker's Island—and set the whole dismal criminal lock-up in Siberia amid the darkest of winters. Good thing for Martia—she warms things up quickly.

Puffing away on a fat, stiletto-like tiparillo, the cat eyed alien offers Kirk a drag, telling him, "It will help keep you warm." It certainly does the trick, but Martia has other more fun ways in which to raise the body temperature. Later, when she plants a kiss on the Captain while he's lying in his bed, it's clear that she'll use every means at her disposal to seduce and manipulate her target.

And then there's that prison kiss.

It doesn't last long. It's no prelude nor foreplay to actual sexual intercourse—after all, Bones would be watching them in the next bed. But it stands out high among the many kisses the Enterprise captain has enlisted over his years of being a laser powered lothario. It's not as culturally important as, say, Uhura and Kirk's tongue hockey in *Plato's Stepchildren*, but maybe because of the ragged state of Kirk's clothing or the dirty, primal prison environ—or just how powerfully seductive Iman is, that kiss provides a fuel to the aging Jim Kirk so much so it lights his face aflame.

Captain Kirk finds that he's completely intrigued with her. Can we blame him? Who wouldn't be? She's also saving his own and his crew mates' hide and she's one hot prison inmate.

But soon thereafter, the fuzzy Tribble poop hits the warp engine core at transwarp speed.

What is it with Kirk and multi gender or hermaphrodite species? Naturally, when you're as big and as successful a player as the good Captain, you're bound to wind up meeting as many different sexually adventurous species as there are to be had by a star hopping starship commander. Still, by now, shouldn't Mr. Enterprise have more of a practiced nose, eye or ear for the many 'fake' humanoids or shape shifters he's encountered over the decades?

Remember that salt loving creature feature? Nancy? How about Garth of Izar? Anyway...

It's soon revealed Martia isn't merely an attractive humanoid at all; she coyly explains, "I thought I'd assume a pleasing shape." In fact, she's likely not even a humanoid at all, or at least she may not be. We're never told nor sure what she truly is, only that she's a Chameloid, and Kirk's definitely heard of the devious race of these crafty body morphers before.

Though the final reveal of her true biological identity offers us cinematic shades of *The Crying Game*, wherein a man is fooled into thinking the male he's falling in love with is really a female, Kirk's dilemma strikes us as far more traumatizing. This isn't just gender confusion – it's a species shell game.

With a transgender or transsexual, at least the actual species isn't in question. After all, Kirk actually kissed her. Kissed Him? It. *That?* Whatever it was, he swapped serious spit with the entity called Martia, and although her exterior forms appear to us completely as a humanoid, Lord knows what's swimming around in the saliva. Hell, maybe Kirk's pregnant now!

No doubt after the good Captain resumed his place in fulfilling those taxing Starfleet duties, tiring himself out from all the many heroic and legendary adventures thereafter, maybe he lulled himself to sleep with this little ditty. After all, green Orion girls are a lot better to play around with than the species undetermined. My apologies to Guns N' Roses:

*Take me down to the Paradise City... Where the **Girls are Green**...*
And the Grass Is Pretty...
Oh, won't you please take me home!

Most Sexually Charged Dialogue Exchange:

Kirk: That's a comfort. I was lucky that thing had knees.

Martia: That was not his knee. Not everyone keeps their genitals in the same place, Captain.

Kirk: Anything you want to tell me?

Kirk & Spock

The Greatest Bromance
of the Galaxy

Bromance: A close, but nonsexual relationship between two men.

"I have been and always shall be your friend." – *Spock to Kirk in ST II: Wrath Of Khan*

Before Han and Luke of *Star Wars*, before Groot and Rocket Raccoon from *Guardians Of The Galaxy*, before Michael and KITT of NBC's *Knight Rider* fame, there was Kirk and Spock. The Starfleet tag team isn't as pulp fiction flashy as roguish Han Solo and Jedi Luke Skywalker, nor as colorful as big, bad Groot or the yappy Rocket Racoon—but it's a good bet Spock could match logical wits with KITT any day of the week and maybe even win.

Judging David Hasselhoff's Michael Knight versus Captain Kirk's charm—*the Hoff VS the Shat*—that's strictly your own personal choice.

Spock's dad Sarek was a full blooded Vulcan. His mom Amanda was a full blooded human being from Earth. This sexual joining of two very different planets meant Kirk's science officer saw things differently than most of his Starfleet peers. Kirk came from a family of Starfleet officers. That may have confined many another man into fitting into a predictable mold, but Cadet Kirk earned a commendation for original thinking when he beat the infamous Kobayashi Maru—Starfleet Academy's 'no win' scenario test.

The Kobayashi Maru phenomenon is something well known to fans. First mentioned in *Wrath of Khan*, it's the dramatic combat simulation given to Starfleet cadets to gauge just how they deal with the many unworkable scenarios they'll surely face when in actual service. How did Kirk pull it off? As his son, David, would bluntly say in *ST:II*, "He cheated."

Today, he'd simply be called a hacker.

Kirk reprogrammed or hacked the brutally challenging exam so he could best it by making it a solvable problem. He changed the rules by any means necessary and overcame the obstacle. How does a free thinker, even a rebellious commanding officer type, find common ground and bond enough with a man who's sought the rules of binding logic to structure his potentially chaotic life?

Opposites attract.

James T. Kirk's an undeniable force of nature, storming in his focused, lifelong quest for wallowing in his emotions. His flaming passion for awesome space exploration, starship battles, unarmed combat, 3D Chess skill, wrestling, martial arts and testing one's mettle, along with his legendary bedroom prowess, paints a compelling picture of a man who wears his heart on his sleeve and conducts his career arc accordingly.

In meeting Spock, Kirk's been set free. He can live vicariously through a logic limiting kind of a lifestyle—where common sense, reason and rigorous scientific method overrule all notions of primal instinct or the impulsive siren call of intuition.

Indeed, one may even observe that in their special relationship— their powerful and loving *bromance*, gender roles are also better defined. Kirk, in certain ways, symbolizes a more feminine thrust—with his emotions and intuition ruling over much of his decision making. The more traditionally masculine realm of calm reason and logic organizing oneself typifies Spock's persona.

Is Kirk now the intuitive chick and Spock the stud?

Fans have always supported *Star Trek* in a special, groundbreaking way. Without the fan letter writing campaign spearheaded by Bjo Trimble back during the original series run, a third broadcast season would likely never have been produced. Today, various fan productions produce near replica episodes of classic *Trek*—complete with cloned props, scripts and actors. *Star Trek* fans are a special breed, indeed.

What about those gay romance stories written by fans?

Fan fiction—before the hoards of YouTube clone episodes—saw dedicated fans pen fantastic tales of NCC-1701 and its crew exploring truly unexplored territory. In some of this fabled 'fanfic', Captain Kirk and Mr. Spock are not simply officers serving aboard the same Federation starship—they are also gay lovers. This fanfic—also known as *Slash*

Fiction—serves up steamy tales of a deep physical love between the two men. Even Gene Roddenberry commented on the notion of physical love or the 'Greek Ideal' and the depiction of the two characters in his show:

> *Yes, there's certainly some of that -- certainly with love overtones. Deep love. The only difference being, the Greek ideal-- we never suggested in the series-- physical love between the two. But it's the- - we certainly had the feeling that the affection was sufficient for that, if that were the particular style of the 23rd century. --* Shatner, William, et al. *Where No Man... The Authorized Biography of William Shatner*

Roddenberry seems to be basically sanctioning a gay coupling of Spock and Kirk—well, if it was in vogue in the 23rd century that is. Despite these 'before their time' sexual suggestions and situations, no fan production has ever encouraged nor depicted the Kirk/Spock or K/S slash fiction meme.

Cloned episodes can be fun, but when it comes to the real deal, you go to the source. It's safe to say that there's one member of the original crew—or more accurately the brilliant actor who brought him to life—who probably wouldn't object to an exploration of a Jim Kirk and Spock homosexual romance. Sulu's heterosexuality was never questioned, but Japanese American actor, George Takei, came out as a gay man.

Oh my! George Takei is now something of a pop culture phenomenon. Even before becoming part of the iconic wacky wack pack of the Howard Stern show on Sirius XM, he was earning his publicity stripes as the hippest original *Trek* cast member this side of Mr. Shatner. He's continued his climb up and right into an ever brighter limelight, along with the public's affection of this veteran Hollywood professional. Takei is a sensitive man and proactive when it comes to social issues and he numbers animal rights and full marriage equality for the LGBT community among his causes.

Apparently, George Takei is now enjoying a time when his voice and his jokes are heard—instead of being relegated to the lower volume background as a supporting player. Now, his impressive public megaphone is social media: He counts well over a million Twitter followers.

It's no secret to followers of Takei's career how much trouble he's had over the years getting along with his flamboyant co-star, William Shatner. The two bickering men make oil and water look like a cozy pair. Behind the scenes tales of Shatner supposedly decreasing the role of Sulu in the feature films—even taking away his key scenes in the script or paring down his lines—are something of a common conversation topic when George Takei plays around with the Stern crew in NYC. Recently, on Conan O'Brien, Takei mocked the overweight Shatner as having no place huffing and puffing down the sets of the J.J. Abrams *Trek* films. He also joked about how ancient Leonard Nimoy looked in the small cameo roles he's had in the movies.

It's more than notable to observe that the one character from the original 'Wagon Train to the stars' with the least amount of on screen sexuality has now became one of the most important new voices in the modern world's take on sexuality in all its diversity and modes of social acceptance: Sulu's crewmates—Chekov, Uhura and Scotty all had some flirtation with romance—yet Sulu never scored.

Evidently, to all who are paying attention and like to keep score, the man who fleshed out Hikaru Sulu back in those less than sexually open or tolerant 1960's, has gotten the last, lusty laugh over his naysayers. These days with legally marrying his longtime partner, Brad, and expanding his role as the go to guy for everything classic *Trek* and beyond, George Takei has been scoring non stop for a good while now.

Oh My, Indeed!

"Galactic Girls"

Trek's Sexiest Women

...or *"How To Select The Sexiest Out Of So Many Candidates"*

"Just imagine what it was like. No engines. No computers. Just the wind and the sea and the stars to guide you."
"Bad food, brutal discipline. No women!"
> – *Captain Picard to Riker and his*
> *reply in Star Trek: Generations*

Are Trekkers fair when it comes to their burning passion? Maybe they're too biased to see past their beloved space warping family when it comes to pants on fire sex appeal. Or, is it just a plain, inarguable fact that *Trek*'s female element glows far more lustily when compared to the rest of sexy sci-fi's feminine elite?

Bones would perhaps simply put it this way, "She's sexy, Jim."

Star Wars boasts sexuality in the form of a scantily clad Princess Leia—at least when the freedom fighting rebel is forced into being a sex slave girl to super spherically obese Jabba The Hutt. How about the many female assistants of BBC's *Doctor Who* over the years? Those girls sure are pretty, but they won't ever make a James Bond girl feel physically inadequate. Let's face it: many space themed romps feature alluring women, but nothing comes close to the sheer raw sex appeal of *Star Trek*.

Trek's gorgeous women make Gene Roddenberry's space opera the sexiest sci-fi show around. From the raw beauty of female Klingon warriors to a supermodel married to a British rock icon—the original Trek to the stars, its movies and TV spin-offs keep bringing sexy back and beyond by showcasing numerous hot space babes.

However, unlike too many lesser storytelling vehicles, these women aren't employed as living set pieces or for cheap eye candy. They are equal players in both action and character. They act in essential capacities—often being fully integral to the plot.

The narratively complex and multi-layered universe which Gene Roddenberry created boasts a cosmic collection of humans, aliens, or often something somewhere in between. The sci-fi phenomenon has showcased the most beautiful, sexy and unreal creatures for five decades now. Among them are alluring Borg babes, seductive casino workers, sexy Starfleet officers and cosmic creations, so incredible and original they defy easy categorization. One thing's for certain: *Star Trek* entices its fan base with some of the sexiest women in the universe—and beyond, right into the multi-verse.

We still live in an age where our beautiful people get most of the media's fawning attention. Coverage of the most interesting or fascinating people may not be a real beauty pageant, but a good deal of the time, it feels like it. *People Magazine* crowns *The Sexiest Man Alive* each year, and that stud of the moment soon becomes the chatty stuff of water cooler fodder: Bradley Cooper, Brad Pitt and Tom Selleck all wore the title at one time. So, one could argue that the gender roles when admiring beauty are nearly equalized—at least in most Western big media. In *Trek*'s prime time heyday, men's looks took a backseat to their striking female counterparts. Taking a cue from that and that American media institution and tradition, *Star Trek* can also crown a few beauties.

Lt. Uhura – Nichelle Nichols & Zoe Saldana – *TOS*

She's no alien.

Nyota Uhura is the communications expert from Earth, who opens hailing frequencies and speaks with real authority to virtually any man, woman, alien or entity anywhere in all parts of the known galaxy. On Roddenberry's classic TV show, Nichelle Nichols fleshed out the role of Lt. Uhura, and she lent a very necessary feminine touch to a program with a mostly male cast. When Spock, Kirk, Dr. McCoy and Scotty needed to send an urgent message, they enlisted this sexy professional.

Re-imaginations bring change. In the re-imagined big budget films from director J.J. Abrams, Zoe Saldana (*Guardians Of The Galaxy*) has taken up the role and continued the legacy of classy sexuality that Nichols created by romancing Zachary Quinto's Spock. These two have been busy setting the whole galaxy aflame with their smoldering romance.

Set your probing phasers on steamy!

Nurse Christine Chapel – Majel Barrett Roddenberry – *TOS*

Nurse, heal thyself—of your crush on the starship's first officer.

Chapel impressed Starfleet brass as a dependable medical professional. She had to, or she would never have been stationed on the prestigious flagship of the space exploring fleet, nor assisted the respected Dr. McCoy, if she was an inefficient quack. With those captivating blue eyes, her blonde locks and a soothing, even sexy voice, Chapel could go from solid and serious to sultry in a flash and beep of a Sickbay bio-bed monitor. Her healthcare knowhow was never in question, however; she suffered from an affliction which could sway her focus: helpless and hapless love for the always stoic Vulcan—Spock.

Actress Majel Barrett would later go on to marry *Trek*'s creator in Japan after the series ended its original broadcast run. Even more importantly to fans, she'd go on to flesh out the wacky Lwaxana Troi on *The Next Generation* as Troi's meddlesome, Betazoid mom, and she'd also provide the Enterprise computer voice for many years to come.

The Borg Queen – Alice Krige – *TNG*

She is the beginning, the end, the one who is many. She brings order to chaos. She is the Borg Queen.

South African actress Alice Krige (*Ghost Story*) slipped into an unimaginably tight cat suit (mostly latex rubber & prosthetics) and both a legendary villain and seductive temptress was born. As the cybernetic villain and ruthless mother hen protecting her Borg brood in the feature film, *Star Trek: First Contact*, Krige nearly tempted Data over to her dark, diva side by promising him the joys of the flesh—literally. *Star Trek: Voyager* featured the return of Krige as the Queen of Borg bad in its final episode. She delighted us in tormenting Captain Kathryn Janeway (Kate Mulgrew) and babe of borg 7of9 (Jeri Ryan), and though apparently she was destroyed in the end, we know just how resourceful – and merciless— she can be when battling her enemies.

Leeta – Chase Masterson – *DS9*

She's the Dabo girl with the delightful difference.

Much like the storytelling prowess of *The Simpsons*, where the supporting characters often outshine the main cast, *Deep Space Nine* brims with recurring actors and actresses who lend so much fun and frolics, you'd want to see a TV show focusing on them alone.

Leeta, employee of Quark's and eventual wife of his brother, the gadget guru Rom (Max Grodenchik), defined an otherworldly sexuality. Actress Chase Masterson infused an irresistible playfulness into her character which endeared her to both fictional residents of station Deep Space Nine—Terok Nor in Cardassian—and the fans who first embraced her as girlfriend to the enigmatic Dr. Bashir, and finally main squeeze of Ferengi Rom. One can only wonder what Leeta is up to these days, now that her hubby calls all the shots as the ruling Grand Nagus.

Yeoman Janice Rand – Grace Lee Whitney – *TOS*

Some have called her 'Captain Kirk's secretary', but any real fan knows that the gorgeous Janice Rand had more than clerical duties on her roster.

Brought to life by actress Grace Lee Whitney (*Some Like It Hot*), Yeoman Rand was the go to gal for Captain Kirk in many capacities. She'd coordinate his duties, bring him his coffee, meals, or make him sign that enormous Padd thingy, years before we called upon our own Android tablets or wiggled a stylus on a iPad. Rand brought a real sense of classic beauty and class to her role and made a difference to the show's first season.

Unfortunately, Whitney was dismissed from the show after only a season, but fans never forgot her ethereal beauty and inescapable sexuality, which made guest stars like the lovesick Charlie Evans (Robert Walker) pine away so miserably for her.

Counselor Deanna Troi – Marina Sirtis – *TNG*

Sometimes a banana is simply a banana. Psychological babble or universal fruity truth? For Counselor Troi on Captain Picard's starship, such aphorisms collided with alien perspectives on a daily basis.

Captain Picard's Enterprise did a lot of things differently from its predecessor, Captain Jim Kirk's Starship. The NCC-1701 D was much larger, far more powerful and allowed family members aboard—including kids—and stationed its own psychological therapist on the bridge. The ship's counselor was a kind of Dr. Joyce Brothers to advise the bridge crew in necessary situations and provide therapeutic respite to the starship family.

Deanna Troi sat alongside Patrick Stewart's (*X-Men: Days of Future Past*) Picard for seven seasons. She was flanked on the other side by her one time love—Commander William (Jonathan Frakes) Riker. Sirtis maintained a professionalism for Troi in her duties and interaction, but when time came to be personal, or even intimate, this excellent actress definitely knew how to turn on the feminine charm.

Vina – Susan Oliver – *TOS*

It isn't easy being green—or so damn sexy. Vina easily puts the red hot in green skin.

Co-starring alongside Jeffrey Hunter (Captain Pike) in the pilot, *The Cage*, which was rejected by NBC, she's the first openly sexual woman featured on *Star Trek*, and still one of its most unforgettable. Many casual *Trek* fans may not know the name of that 'sexy green gal' when they see a photo still or the episode, but they can never forget her.

Vina—with the illusory help of powerful telepathic zookeepers, the Talosians—can appear as any woman, but all with an incendiary sexual energy. From intellectual scientist assistant to the landing party and survivors who never were, to the smoldering Orion Slave Girl dancing up an erotic storm for an entranced Christopher Pike on a faraway world, to the prim and proper girlfriend on a picnic in the pastoral environs of Earth, Vina truly defines the sheer sexual power of Gene Roddenberry's incredibly sexually mature universe.

Martia – Iman – *Star Trek VI: The Undiscovered Country*

Rock icon David Bowie gets to kiss Captain Kirk's prison love.

As an internationally known supermodel in the ultra competitive world of fashion, Iman knows a lot about what it takes to be uber sexy. Originally, *Trek VI* screenwriter Denny Martin Flinn conceived the character of Martia as a tough, female space pirate. He even envisioned Hollywood A-Lister Sigourney Weaver (*Aliens*) fleshing out the role. Who could blame him? Weaver practically invented the tough, and resourceful, but still feminine space ace with her turn in British director Ridley Scott's classic sci-fi thriller, *Alien*. But in the perfect casting of Iman, the producers gave us a decidedly different kind of cosmic criminal.

With those catlike, yellow eyes and her exotic alien accent (her own native accent), Martia is one sexually mature creature ready for anything. That she's also a crafty shape shifter—and can change her height, weight, body hair amount and even gender nearly instantaneously—makes her one of the most versatile sexy women in the galaxy.

Lt. Jadzia Dax – Terry Farrell – *DS9*

How many lives can one person lead?

Star Trek: Deep Space Nine is the 2nd spin-off to Gene Roddenberry's classic science fiction saga. Set against the backdrop of complex political intrigue, double dealing and genuine mysticism, *DS9* introduced us to a whole new crew—a mix of Starfleet stalwarts and hardened law upholders like mysterious Constable Odo, the station's chief of security, played by Rene Auberjonois.

Commander Benjamin Sisko (Avery Brooks) delighted in having an old friend as his new science officer. The catch? His buddy used to be a *guy*. Now, his old bud's mind, memories, soul or his *katra* has been implanted into the body of a sultry humanoid from an alien race called Trill.

We like to colorfully point to a person's career as having many facets, phases or even lives, but for the Trill, it's literally the case. Beautiful actress Terry Farrell—who was also a top model—created this complex character of combination humanoid beauty host with a slug-like symbiotic creature residing within her. The symbiont, worm-like slug had lived for centuries retaining memories of previous humanoid hosts, who would eventually die and then be replaced with a new host.

Dr. Carol Marcus – Bibi Besch – *Star Trek II: Wrath Of Khan*

Was Jim Kirk ever a boy scout? Nah. Not according to his first love, one Dr. Marcus.

In the second feature film outing for the original TV cast, *Star Trek II: The Wrath of Khan*, Admiral Kirk must deal with a dual blast from the past. It seems a maniacal despot from Earth's past, seething with vengeance, is now free from the planet Kirk marooned him on. Also, apparently, his son borne of his pairing with Dr. Carol Marcus hates his guts.

No problem. Easy. All in a day's work for the inimitable Starship Captain J.T. Kirk.

Actress Bibi Besch (*Police Story*) brings a stunning physical quality to her role as Kirk's old flame. She smoothly exudes the confidence and intellectual curiosity required to be the scientist mother of the awe inspiring **Genesis Device**—a gadget which literally remakes the matter of entire worlds into whatever its programmed matrix designates, while also letting us know just why Kirk dated her. Carol Marcus also appears in the big screen re-imagination—*Star Trek: Into Darkness*—this time played by British actress Alice Eve.

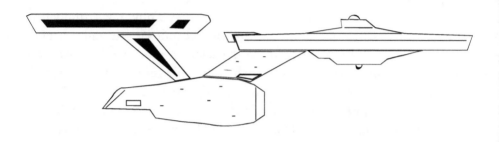

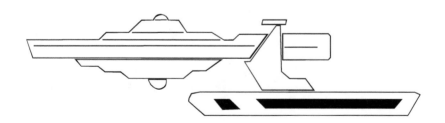

Starship Sexy
Trek's Sexiest Starships

"USS Enterprise shakedown cruise report. I think this 'new' ship was put together by monkeys. Oh, she's got a fine engine, but half the doors won't open, and guess whose job it is to make it right?"
-- Scotty in ST V: The Final Frontier.

Sorry, Scotty, but you know this better than most: The complex and fabled *Star Trek* universe isn't only about ships named Enterprise. Though top of the Starfleet line, your precious 'bairns' aren't the only warp capable game in town.

Star Trek Sex is a fun celebration of all things sexual connected with classic *Star Trek*. In that spirit, how could we overlook the very vehicles which make all the fast, flying future fun possible? After all, Kirk was always so committed and loyal to his lady Enterprise, it was as if he was married to her all the same.

Gene Roddenberry knew just how magical the starship setting could be. The former military and commercial pilot was well versed in just how connected a captain and crew could become to the flying machine which ferried them around at super fast velocities. Here's how *Trek*'s father regarded the Starship Enterprise.

"The Starship Enterprise is not a collection of motion picture sets or a model used in visual effects. It is a very real vehicle, one designed for storytelling. You the audience furnish its propulsion. With a wondrous leap of imagination, you make it into a real spaceship that can take us into the far reaches of the galaxy and sometimes even the depths of the human soul."

Roddenberry penned this as part of the introduction to *TNG*'s FX and art directors Rick Sternbach and Mike Okuda's fan favorite book—*Star Trek: The Next Generation Technical Manual*. Sure, it's a safe bet that Roddenberry's wagon train to the stars will always be led into the unknown most famously by the Starship Enterprise. The starship was first under the command of Captain Pike, then Captain Kirk. Later on in the next generation, it fell under the command of Captain Jean-Luc Picard. Starships named Enterprise show themselves over and over to be favored ships indeed.

However, even the greatest ship or most able crew can't do it all alone. Among the history of *Star Trek* television series and feature films, there are many other starships. Warp speed vessels, which distinguished themselves in valiant battle or thrilling exploration. Here are other Starfleet starships and those who piloted them.

USS Intrepid NCC-1831

There were other ships like Enterprise featured in the original series. And while this one may not come under the heading of truly sexy, the dark chapter of its appearance is unforgettable.

This was also a Constitution class vessel like its sister ship the USS Enterprise. In the original series episode, *The Immunity Syndrome*, an enormous single celled organism, like some mammoth amoeba, destroys the Intrepid.

What's most disturbing about the story and the ship's destruction is that Spock senses the all Vulcan crew of about 400 dying as the ship is destroyed. Spock's shocking revelation gave us an idea of how powerful his race was in terms of mental connection. The scene remains one of the most chilling and powerfully dramatic moments in the entire *Star Trek* mythology.

USS Reliant NCC-1864

Under the command of Captain Terrell in the 1982 hit movie *Star Trek II: The Wrath of Khan*, the USS Reliant was primarily a science vessel of exploration and discovery.

Dr. Carol Marcus, former flame of Captain Kirk, was head of the Genesis Project, which needs a planet devoid of life to initiate experimentation. An away team composed of Terrell and first office Chekov discover far too late that they've landed on the wrong planet. Instead of Ceti Alpha VI, they are on Ceti Alpha V, a planet on which many years earlier Captain Kirk, under order of Starfleet Command, had imprisoned Khan Noonian Soong, the villainous genetic superman of a past war torn Earth.

The superior minded, egotistical Khan manages to take control of Reliant and to engage his old enemy Kirk in battle. The space battles between the two old enemies which ensue are still considered by many fans as some of the best and most fun in Star Trek. They may not have the pixel puffery of today's digital laden feasts, but the men (actors) behind the phaser and photon fire seem to eclipse the video game wonder of more modern movies.

USS Excelsior NX-2000

Known as the 'great experiment', this vessel had a breakthrough in starship warp speed technology called transwarp.

First showcased in *Star Trek III: The Search For Spock*, then later in *Star Trek VI: The Undiscovered Country* under the command of Captain Sulu, the Excelsior was a sleekly designed and powerful starship. If starship sexy could be encapsulated justly, the Excelsior would be at the head of the pack.

One of the more comedic moments in *ST III* concerned Scotty sabotaging the ship's engines by removing essential hardware. When the Excelsior tries to chase after Kirk, who 'borrows' the Enterprise from space dock, the Excelsior sputters weakly to a stop as the Enterprise jumps away into warp and escapes.

USS Defiant NX-74205

The Defiant is a tough, little ship with a lot of power. Starfleet, being a non-military organization of explorers at its core, finally made something more resembling a battleship for high level defense in response to a rampaging alien threat.

Making its debut in the third season of *Star Trek: Deep Space Nine*, this starship was developed as a powerful defense against the Borg threat looming over the Federation. Station DS9 Commander Benjamin Sisko participated in Defiant's design, which was fitting since he lost his wife Jennifer in the infamous Borg battle of Wolf 359. Sisko never did take the

Defiant into battle against the Borg, but the Klingon Worf did to great fanfare in the movie, *Star Trek: First Contact*.

USS Voyager NCC-74656

Captain Kathryn Janeway (Kate Mulgrew) was the first female captain featured on a *Star Trek* series and her vessel was another first by being a strikingly different class of Starship and not of the Enterprise lineage.

Voyager boasted a sleeker design than other Starships, a reduced crew size and internal circuitry enhanced by bio-neural gel packs; a kind of living computer based on an organic brain. On a mission to stop a ter-rorist group called the Maquis, Voyager followed the rebel band into a strange sector of space known as the Badlands. Subsequently, they were tossed 70,000 light years into the Delta Quadrant by an enigmatic super alien called the Caretaker.

It may be debatable to some, but it's been said that it's rare that any-thing can be sexier than pure thought. After all, what makes sex sexy? Keeping that in mind, Voyager's incredible computer system alone – the bio-neural gel circuits – make the ship a sexy one for certain. Brawny ar-mament aside, Voyager made do with a much more lithe way of processing information. In a firefight, that's not only sexy, but tactically advantageous.

Klingon Bird Of Prey

It's not so unusual for the bad guys to have the sexiest guns.

First seen in the third big screen feature film, *Search For Spock*, the Bird of Prey is the battleship workhorse of the Klingon Empire. These predatory space birds catch both the eye and the soul of the true warrior.

Sleek, speedy and full of deadly offensive weapons, guns, guns and more guns, the warping space birds make up for their lack of physical brawn with excellent maneuverability and by employing that most crafty of tech gadgets—borrowed from the Romulans—the infamous cloaking device. By the time one of these cloaked ships comes screaming out of its invisibility cloak to lay down firepower, it may be far too late for a Federation ship to respond. In *ST VI*, General Chang utilized a Bird Of Prey which could fire while cloaked—something never seen employed in battle ever before.

Lt. Uhura
Sexual Strategy

Hailing frequencies open. Incoming transmission. Translation matrix active.

Acting as head communications officer, starship translator and unofficial Chief Musical Officer of the Enterprise—she'd sing and play instruments—actress Nichelle Nichols fleshed out Lt. Nyota Uhura into an indispensable part of Captain Kirk's crackerjack bridge crew team. She blazed a pop culture trail as the only female bridge officer and the only main cast African American performer on Gene Roddenberry's ground breaking trek to the stars.

If you polled even a casual Trekker (*Star Trek* fan) on who they felt were the more sexually capable, mature and or even overall sexually active characters on the classic TV show, Kirk, Spock and Pavel Chekov would no doubt top the list. *Aye, me laddie,* even Scotty would come in there somewhere. Indeed, he and Uhura do get pretty close in one of the feature films. But the simple truth is that the Starfleet professional and alluring singer and dancer, Uhura, had more than a few memorable sexual laced escapades.

Employing and exploring one's sexuality as a lure or naughty temptation, or in Captain Kirk's case, an almost chronic hobby in and out of personal quarters, isn't only a game for the Starfleet boys.

The Man Trap

The first *Trek* episode broadcast would serve as one of the first genuine showcases of just how sexually adventurous the landmark sci-fi series would eventually become. Although the episode heavily focuses on Dr. McCoy's old flame, a pleasant, though mildly disturbing Nancy Crater, there's a scene set aboard the Enterprise involving Uhura which is one of the spooky tale's more memorable and creepy moments.

The vampire-like Salt Creature, who instead of thirsting for blood, feeds on the biochemical sodium chloride compounds and salts found within living organisms, is on the loose on Starship Enterprise. Crazed for more salty snacks, it finds its way to coming in contact with the communications officer. Bumping into Lt. Uhura in one of the ship's corridors, the beast attempts to make her comfortable—and even flirt with her—by assuming the form of an attractive human male. To make things even more familiar and interesting to the bridge officer, the shape shifting monster probes her mind and has the man speak Swahili to her—which is her own native dialect.

Uhura becomes so completely captivated by the predatory shape shifter, she acts like some helpless fly caught in a mentally projected neural web. However, instead of forced bondage and torturous imprisonment, the trap being woven about her is clearly a pleasant, enjoyable one. It's honey and sugar for the fly. The creature is so skilled at seducing humans at the most basic level, it's like Uhura's been slammed with a powerful love potion. Ultimately, the salt loving thing never gets its suckers on Enterprise's communications officer, and McCoy's old flame will forever be linked with a two legged octopus-like salt junkie.

After the haunting episode end credits roll, loyal viewers know very little about the shape shifting alien beast and probably don't really care. We do, however, apparently get more of a glimpse into Lt. Uhura as a person and even as a romantic woman. Since the creature projects the ideal mate or date into its potential prey's mind, we now have more of a notion—albeit one under the duress of a mental attack—of the kind of man who attracts Uhura.

The man who appears to her, spun from the beast's deadly charms, is gentle, handsome and seems familiar to her. Is this the most common strategy when the creature is pursuing a new target? Or, is Lt. Nyota Uhura a woman who yearns for a partner she can relate to on many levels—both physical and culturally. Evidently, for her—at least in this stage in her dynamic life as cosmic explorer of the space ways—opposites don't attract.

Mirror, Mirror

Who says Starfleet duty doesn't have its romantic perks? Put in enough time as a member of the UFP's exploratory force of highly trained professionals, and you just may find something akin to *Fifty Shades of Grey*. What's even better is you'll be engaged in the line of duty. No worries about getting reprimanded for flirting on your own free time.

It may not be the official shore leave tagline, but it's more a case of understanding that: *What happens in Starfleet, stays in Starfleet.*

That ever dependable gadget, the mystical, near magical transporter, can not only ferry landing parties and away teams to other planets in the sparkle of an eye, but zap one into parading and playing around in alternate universes. Once there, you'll get a taste of just how the other half lives—in this case, how they love, tempt, connive, tease and play.

Yet again, Uhura must play on the same playing field as her male counterparts, and not only does she hold her own, she pulls off a number of the most memorable scenes in the fan favorite tale.

No matter if alternate dimensions or universes, or time travel for that matter, are ever proven or utilized by humanity, the science fiction world trades in the plot devices which allow us to explore so many *what-if* scenarios. What if you went back in time and met your younger self? What if you flashed forward and witnessed your own death?

What if a mirror reality beckoned where you were not the same kind of person?

Uhura must swiftly adjust to an Enterprise where civility, manners and personal boundaries are as meaningless and quaint as using drums of oil or rocket fuel and combustion engines for ship propulsion.

And she must also deal with a lusty, savage Sulu, on the prowl after her.

Uhura isn't a woman one should ever underestimate—no matter what side of the universe she's operating in or on what Enterprise she's serving as acting communications officer. That this 'mirror' Sulu doesn't take this into account is his big mistake.

After playing a little cat and mouse game of flirtation, to buy the rest of her crew time to prep tech things to get back home, Uhura smacks the horny helmsman in the face and whips out a dagger which is all business. Sulu is shocked, but he backs off and Uhura escapes into the turbolift.

Kirk couldn't have done it any better by seducing one of his many alien space babes.

Star Trek V: *The Final Frontier*

Uhura and Spock are a steamy item in the cinematic *Trek* re-inventions from director J.J. Abrams. *Star Trek* (2009) and *Star Trek: Into Darkness* (2013) are the big box office action heavy Treks. They mix and match our familiar Enterprise characters. The more aware and geekier amongst the audience cling to the fact that this 'reboot' is relating adventures from an 'alternate timeline'—or an alternate reality which means they can basically change anything.

Whatever.

If the romantic pairing of the laid back Vulcan male and the musical human female came as a surprise to some long time fans, what if Scotty and Uhura got hot and heavy? Well, it sort of happened in this feature film.

The Final Frontier is an odd movie in many respects. First and foremost, it's an odd numbered Trek, and that never bodes well at the outset. I, III and V are all viewed as less than stellar cosmic rides. With the fifth big trek fest, things got so odd, the crew went near evangelical—as in searching for God.

STV isn't going to appear on any fan's 'best of *Trek*'. Directed by Bill Shatner, it's widely recognized as the weakest critically – 21% on Rotten Tomatoes—and least popular among fans of the original series of feature films. Bogged down by an arguably preposterous plot and poor production values, it's a Trek most fans wouldn't brag about when discussing their beloved franchise with the unwashed rabble of the uninitiated—or worst of all, a rabid *Star Wars* fan who's still going through a second or third childhood burdened with that darned lightsaber fetish. Still, despite its myriad of flaws, to see a ranting, raving and emotionally charged Vulcan Sybok (Laurence Luckinbill) preach about finding a paradisiacal Eden and even God almighty himself, does have its share of memorable on screen moments.

Scotty is Starfleet's master of high tech goodness. He's the groovy gadget guru of the 23rd century. He's the real time Radio Shack rugrat. Let's be honest—Scotty's an uber nerd. In fairness, the Mr. Fix-It of Enterprise NCC-1701 never cut a figure as compelling as, say, Sean Connery's James Bond or Harrison Ford's Indy, but in most categories Montgomery Scott in his prime wasn't too hard on the eyes. Unfortunately, he definitely hasn't aged all too well physically from the glory days of that aborted five year mission. We can attribute his great girth to far too many trips to the replicator while working his adored engines into the wee hours of the evening.

When we see him waddling around in the fifth silver screen go round of the venerable Enterprise crew, he's not exactly the fit, suave romantic man archetype. So, it's no surprise that when Uhura, fresh from a motivational speak with Sybok—the Tony Robbins of the known universe—shoots a kindly eye at Mr. Scott, anyone watching may be perplexed.

It's the kind of eye from which romance grows and gets folk smack dab into the dating game. When Uhura springs her flirtatious charms on Scotty, as he comes to consciousness in Sickbay, it's pretty shocking indeed—at least for him. We must remember that Uhura isn't herself during this attack of unbridled passion. She's been liberated by a mighty confidence builder—the laughing Vulcan himself.

She tries to explain things and put him at ease. "Scotty, dear, he's not a madman. Sybok has simply put us in touch with feelings that we've always been afraid to express."

Scotty knows Uhura isn't warping along on both nacelles and tries his best to leave. But Uhura won't be denied. She slams him roughly back down on the bed and says lustily to him, "There's so much I want to tell you." Scotty pities her. He caresses Uhura's face in a paternal or brotherly manner, trying his best to wait out and ward off the temporary love spell she's laboring under, but she responds more like his girlfriend.

If Uhura is right about Sybok, and throughout the movie, we see him liberate other crew members of their secret burdens or emotionally laden pains—refreshing their tired souls with a new focus of honesty and truth—then evidently, Uhura has been pining away for Scotty for awhile now.

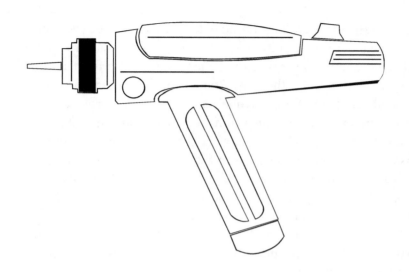

Star Trek Sex, Pop Culture & Howard Stern

To Boldly Go Where No Comic Has Gone Before...

From early on after its three year original broadcast run, Captain Kirk and crew were immortalized in the American pop culture tapestry with both loving tribute and biting satire. If not the record holder for most comic take-offs on any one TV show, it's certainly safely in the top ten of the hall of parody fame.

In 1976, *The Last Voyage Of The Enterprise* warped into classic laugh-fest history, as a hilarious comedy skit. The NBC comedy powerhouse *Saturday Night Live*, network home to the original series run, showcased John Belushi as Kirk, Chevy Chase as Mr. Spock and Dan Aykroyd as the miracle worker engineer Montgomery 'Scotty' Scott. Guest star El-liot Gould played an NBC TV executive intent on getting his hands on the props—phasers, tricorders, communicators, etc.—including Spock's pointy Vulcan ears, to replicate them for merchandising and toys. When the legendary ears are ripped off of Chase, he stutters around briefly in total puzzlement, then bursts into a tantrum of tears.

Animation Fascination

In animation, everyone can hear you scream—and laugh, burp, fart, sneeze...

101

FOX's *The Simpsons, Futurama and Family Guy* have made something of a regular creative sideline with so many *Trek* jabs and romps. From quickie references and ribald jokes, to lampooning full on entire episodes, these animated hit shows may be responsible for more *Star Trek* satire than anything ever seen in live action. Adding to the fun is the fact that often the *Trek* stars themselves join in on the chuckles by appearing on the program and lending their voice to their animated counterparts.

The raw and wild writers of Seth MacFarlane's *Family Guy* in particular have poked some real adult fun at *Trek*. They consistently get big names like Patrick Stewart, Jonathan Frakes and Wil Wheaton to authenticate the parody parade. George Takei, the original Sulu from TOS, has also participated in a plethora of Sulu inspired frolic.

Of course Takei's career has been in an upswing, and one of the other gigs which has given him a renaissance in pop culture is acting as the official narrator or voice over guy for a certain radio show host or shock jock.

Howard Stern & Klingon Sex

Oh my!—George Takei

The King of All Media dearly loves his *Star Trek*. Howard Stern, an iconic radio pioneer and celebrated author, movie and TV star is an unabashed comic book and sci-fi geek. Stern not only goes on and on about sci-fi and genre stuff like *The Walking Dead, X-Men, Spider-Man or Star Trek*, but he shares his geek love with his buddy and make-up guy, Ralph. Stern also calls Ralph his boyfriend—but that's a whole other sordid story.

Over the years, Stern and his crack wack pack have had *Trek* luminaries like William Shatner and Jimmy Doohan in the studio, and they'd tell fun stories about the days of playing and filming on the original sets at Desilu. However, most of the supporting players wouldn't exactly have the nicest things to say about the Canadian actor who first fleshed out James T. Kirk back in 1966.

Stern and his ever elegant sidekick Robin Quivers would tease Shatner about how all of his co-stars seemed to not like him—OK they HATED Shatner—and Shatner would either pretend or genuinely not comprehend why his starship crew couldn't get behind their commander in real life.

And then George 'Mr. Sulu' Takei was invited onto the craziest show on the airwaves.

At first, Takei wanted no part of Stern, Fred, Benjy, Sal or Robin in the beginning, and the crazy gang even irritated him more when they spoofed him by pretending to be Ricardo Montalban (Khan himself) and calling the unsuspecting Japanese American actor for a prank fest. Takei was mega annoyed at first by the attention Stern and his fans gave him, but then realized that all that loving adoration wasn't put on—it was for real. It wasn't a joke, it wasn't a cheap insult. It was real love for George Takei and helmsman Sulu in *Star Trek*.

Stern fans catch Howard on satellite radio Sirius XM. Listeners can be treated to lots of fun *Star Trek* references. Among those silly bits, there are also graphic sexual situations. Before we delve into that deviltry, I have a personal story that fits right in with Stern and *Trek*.

Hatred is seldom constructive. Sure, we may hate lima beans, but culinary hate only insults canned veggies or clueless cooks whipping up limp lima. When hatred interferes with something as exciting as a TV interview, it's simply embarrassing for the one doing the hating. For me, the hater was former CNN correspondent and author Jack Cafferty—once a local news anchor for NYC's WPIX. Cafferty's hate for Howard Stern threatened to derail my *Star Trek: The Next Generation* TV interview.

Bill Clinton was President, and I'd just sold my first TV script to Paramount Pictures. Scoring my first writing sale for the legendary franchise was the stuff of dreams. When my school, Ramapo College of NJ, coordinated an interview with Channel 11 WPIX, it turned even more dreamy. Little did I know Jack Cafferty would seek to turn my dream into a nightmare.

Although a local New York City station, WPIX, benefits from 'super station' status, it's also carried by satellite in other markets. When the news department called to confirm, they told me my interview wouldn't be only seen in NYC, but all over America. The same day a massive earthquake hit LA, so there was doubt about whether a 'color' piece on a local boy making good in Hollywood could be run amid the west coast turmoil. Finally, the interview was a go, and the Cafferty oddity began.

WPIX sent reporter Jason Carroll. Jason's a great guy and he's now Cafferty's CNN colleague. Co-anchor Kaity Tong would do my introduction. Everything was set, except I unknowingly owned an item Mr. Cafferty would strongly object to being seen on his newscast. Howard had recently written his blockbuster bio, *Private Parts*. It was the must get book for Stern fans and pop culture aficionados alike. A buddy had gifted me with the hilarious volume, and I prominently displayed it near the PC I used to write my TNG script.

While the camera crew set up, Jason checked with the studio through his earpiece and things still proceeded smoothly, until he began looking worriedly at my Stern book.

"That must be removed from the shot," he said.

"Why?" I replied. This was getting weird.

Jason paused, listening to his ear piece. "Jack... He... *They* don't want it in the shot."

As a Howard Stern fan for years, I knew there was no love lost between Stern and Cafferty. Details of their dust-ups escape me, but Cafferty and Stern were broadcasters made to hate each other. Now, Jack Cafferty wanted me to remove Howard's bestseller from being seen in the TV interview of my life.

I thought, "Oh, hell no!"

"If the book goes, there's no interview." I meant it. Talk about sticking up for your comic idol, but this was also principle. I felt strongly the request was beneath anyone to ask, and certainly was far too silly for me to grant. The book remained. My interview went off smoothly. Jack Cafferty survived seeing the book of his nemesis in the shot.

Among the best and funniest comic bits have to be the obscene Klingon sex phone calls with Robin. Listening to them has us convinced that Robin is a Klingon language expert—at least while she's in the sack.

Robin Quivers, by any logical or class measure analysis, should not be mixing it up with the high school shenanigans of Stern's sex maniacs. Quivers is an authentic intellectual—a military woman and a registered nurse—and her interests and expertise fairly outshine a dozen women in her peer group or beyond. But that's just what makes her inclusion in Howard Stern's world so pitch perfect.

Robin plays den mother with a lilting laugh which keeps the boys mostly in check—without stifling the comic vibe that makes the Howard Stern party so original and fun. Her contributions can't be overlooked or undervalued and her Klingon phone sex sessions only add to her unique charm.

Yes, Klingon sex.

It seems that Robin enjoys speaking Klingon and she appears to obsess on speaking Klingon words that sound awfully like the English term for a penis. The gang also love to call up Chinese restaurants armed with Robin speaking Klingon, so she can order up something really alien for a lunch special to make even galley expert Neelix proud.

"Cock is on your mind when you speak Klingon," Stern quipped to Robin on a recent show, after listening to a recording of her solemnly intoning the language of Kahless, Kang and Worf. She rattles off the words like a real trooper. Robin Quivers may not be a true Klingon language expert, nor ever swing a Bat'leth proudly, but it's no doubt she could probably seduce a Klingon warrior or two into her bed anytime.

In the spirit of Howard & Robin... *Live Long & Penis.*

Q'apla!

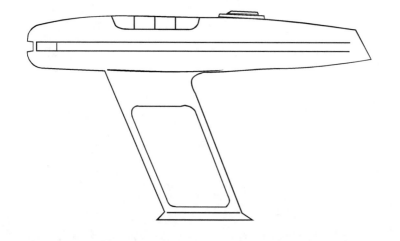

The Episodes

The Cage
Director: Robert Butler
Airdate: 11.27.88—TV premier after being previously released on VHS tape on 10.14.86

Where No Man Has Gone Before
Director: James Goldstone
Airdate: 9.22.66

The Man Trap
Director: Marc Daniels
Airdate: 9.8.66

Charlie X
Director: Lawrence Dobkin
Airdate: 9.15.66

The Naked Time
Director: Marc Daniels
Airdate: 9.29.66

The Enemy Within
Director: Leo Penn
Airdate: 10.6.66

Mudd's Women
Director: Harvey Hart
Airdate: 10.13.66

What Are Little Girls Made Of?
Director: James Goldstone
Airdate: 10.20.66

Miri
Director: Vincent McEveety
AirDate: 10.27.66

The Return of the Archons
Director: Joseph Pevney
AirDate: 2.9.67

Space Seed
Director: Marc Daniels
AirDate: 2.16.67

This Side Of Paradise
Director: Ralph Senenesky
AirDate: 3.2.67

The City On The Edge Of Forever
Director: Joseph Pevney
AirDate: 4.6.67

Amok Time
Director: Joseph Pevney
AirDate: 9.15.67

Who Mourns For Adonais?
Director: Marc Daniels
AirDate: 9.22.67

Mirror, Mirror
Director: Marc Daniels
AirDate: 10.6.67

The Apple
Director: Joseph Pevney
AirDate: 10.13.67

Metamorphosis
Director: Ralph Senenesky
AirDate: 11.10.67

Wolf In The Fold
Director: Joseph Pevney
AirDate: 12.22.67

The Trouble With Tribbles
Director: Joseph Pevney
AirDate: 12.69.67

Assignment: Earth
Director: Marc Daniels
AirDate: 3.29.68

The Enterprise Incident
Director: John Meredyth Lucas
AirDate: 9.27.68

Is There In Truth No Beauty?
Director: Ralph Senenesky
AirDate: 10.18.68

A Private Little War
Director: Marc Daniels
AirDate: 2.2.68

By Any Other Name
Director: Marc Daniels
AirDate: 2.23.68

For The World Is Hollow and I Have Touched The Sky
Director: Tony Leader
AirDate: 11.8.68

Plato's Stepchildren
Director: David Alexander
AirDate: 11.22.68

Wink Of An Eye
Director: Jud Taylor
AirDate: 11.29.68

The Empath
Director: John Erman
AirDate: 12.6.68

Elaan Of Troyius
Director: John Meredyth Lucas
AirDate: 12.20.68

Whom Gods Destroy
Director: Herb Wallerstein
AirDate: 1.3.69

The Mark of Gideon
Director: Jud Taylor
AirDate: 1.17.69

The Gamesters of Triskelion
Director: Gene Nelson
AirDate: 1.5.68

Requiem for Methuselah
Director: Murray Golden
AirDate: 2.14.69

The Way To Eden
Director: David Alexander
AirDate: 2.21.69

All Our Yesterdays
Director: Marvin Chomsky
AirDate: 3.14.69

Turnabout Intruder
Director: Herb Wallerstein
AirDate: 6.3.69

Movies

Star Trek: The Motion Picture
Director: Robert Wise
Release Date: 1979

Star Trek V: The Final Frontier
Director: William Shatner
Release Date: 1989

Star Trek VI: The Undiscovered Country
Director: Nicholas Meyer
Release Date: 1991

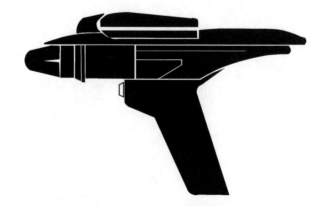

Image Gallery

Credit: NBC Television
Copyright: Wikimedia Commons/public domain

Credit: NBC Television
Copyright: Wikimedia Commons/public domain

Credit: Will Stape
Copyright: 2007

Credit: Will Stape
Copyright: 2007

Credit: Will Stape
Copyright: 2007

Index

CPSIA information can be obtained
at www.ICGtesting.com
Printed in the USA
BVHW040627170619
551160BV00007B/72/P